Tomb Travel

A guide to Northern Ireland's megalithic monuments

Harry Welsh

©Northern Ireland Environment Agency 2011

Applications for reproduction should be made in writing to the Stationery Office Ltd, St Crispins, Duke Street, Norwich, NR3 1PD.

The information contained in this publication is believed to be correct at time of manufacture. Whilst care has been taken to ensure that the information is accurate, the publisher can accept no responsibility for any errors or omissions or for changes to the details given.

The contributors assert their moral rights under the Copyright, Designs and Patents Act 1988, to be identified as authors of this work.

A CIP catalogue record for this book is available from the British Library.

A Library of Congress CIP catalogue record has been applied for.

First published 2011

ISBN 978 0 337 09684 6

Published by The Stationery Office

Editorial services by Editorial Solutions (Ireland) Ltd, designed by LSD Limited and printed in Northern Ireland by GPS Colour Graphics

Contents

Foreword

Northern Ireland's megalithic tombs rank among our most ancient monuments – many date back almost 6,000 years into our past. They embody the first locally based evidence of mankind erecting permanent structures upon our landscape. Indeed, they represent the start of a long architectural heritage that connects with and reaches forward through time to the buildings of today.

As an architect, megalithic monuments hold a particular fascination for me. On visiting tombs such as Creggandevesky, County Tyrone, the Kempe Stones, County Down or Ballymacdermot, County Armagh, I am struck with the notion that I am confronting the evidence of the work of fellow 'architects' from the dawn of what we may view as civilisation on our island. These are structures that have been carefully thought out, constructed and used. They have been designed and built in a chosen location for a specific purpose. Once you grasp those facts it is hard not to stand at such sites and feel a direct and very tangible link to our ancestors and the past that has helped shape the north of Ireland of today. It is also fascinating to consider that many of our megalithic monuments were already over one thousand years old when the pharaohs were creating the pyramids in Egypt.

Thus megaliths are an important part of our cultural heritage and it is my ardent hope that this book will encourage (and enable) you to go out and experience these sites for yourself. There are hundreds of megalithic monuments throughout Northern Ireland. However, we have chosen here to concentrate on the smaller number that the Northern Ireland Environment Agency owns or is the guardian of. Our members of staff are rightly proud of the protection and preservation work they do on your behalf and are very pleased to show off these heritage treasures to the world. In doing so we also recognise that this is done not only for 'pure' heritage purposes, but also as an aid to improving health and wellbeing along with the economic benefits to our tourist industry and our local communities.

Many of us have visited far off places, and discovered the sights – and sites – there, but all too often we have not visited the impressive places in our own landscape.

I hope that this publication will help to redress some of that imbalance and stimulate more repeat visits by the intrepid group that has been there before.

The information and directions in the 'Tomb Travelling' section should help guide your way county by county.

In an era of cutbacks and all too often increasing costs it is good to note that access is free of charge.

Thank you for buying this book – I wish you many fascinating hours of exploration and enjoyment.

Michael D A Coulter
Director: Built Heritage

Greengraves Portal Tomb, County Down

Acknowledgements

In an entry level book on the subject of megalithic tombs the writer is required to leave out many of the references to books, articles and sources that helped form the work. I trust anyone who recognises their input here will appreciate this necessity.

I would like to thank the following persons:

At the Northern Ireland Environment Agency: Built Heritage, Paul Logue, Dr Brian Williams and Gail Pollock and Dr John O'Keeffe who were involved in various ways in commissioning and facilitating the publication of this book. I would also thank Dr Chris Lynn for commenting on an early version of the book and Gareth Edwards for sourcing many of the images.

At the Queen's University of Belfast: Professor James Mallory, School of Geography, Archaeology and Palaeoecology, who provided guidance and comment on the various drafts of this publication. Professor Mallory is a respected authority on Irish prehistory and it was a privilege and pleasure to work with him. Also, Professors Paula Reimer and Mike Baillie, who provided details of the development of radiocarbon and dendrochronology at the university. Dr Colm Donnelly and the staff of the Centre for Archaeological Fieldwork, School of Geography, Archaeology and Palaeoecology, gave freely of their experience and expertise on prehistoric sites throughout Ireland.

Paul Walsh, Department of the Environment, Heritage and Local Government (DoEHLG), for facilitating access to the national archives of the Republic of Ireland and advice and information on the classification of megalithic tombs and other prehistoric burial monuments.

June Welsh and Anne MacDermott of the Ulster Archaeological Society, for their enthusiastic support and assistance in connection with this publication.

Clontygora Court Tomb, County Armagh

The Truth About Tombs

The Truth About Tombs

Northern Ireland has a beautiful landscape, richly endowed with a historic monuments and buildings. We are lucky to have so many historic sites and monuments from almost all known periods of human activity here. You can get out and see them in all parts of the country. They are attractive, interesting, and sometimes mysterious destinations, for local people and visitors from around the world to study and enjoy.

Many of these places, like Carrickfergus Castle in County Antrim, are beautifully preserved and easy to see, get to and enjoy. Northern Ireland's megalithic tombs are an important group of ancient sites too. But they aren't quite so prominent and easy to get to, and most are located in out-of-the-way parts of the countryside.

Of course the truth is that megalithic tombs are the oldest-surviving historic structures in Northern Ireland; potent prehistoric survivors of our ancient past and something of a hidden national treasure. We are extremely fortunate that many of these monuments, hugely important to our historical landscape and cultural heritage, have been preserved for the enjoyment of present and future generations.

When you travel to these tombs you will be frequently rewarded with spectacular views over the surrounding countryside. They are inspirational and instil wonder at the achievements of our prehistoric ancestors. And they are smashing locations for a day out.

The word megalithic comes from two Greek words megas (great) and lithos (stone). It describes a variety of monuments built using very large stones. In Northern Ireland these monuments range from single standing stones to complex structures that contain different features like stone galleries and passages.

When archaeologists talk about megalithic tombs, they are referring to large stone-built structures in which human remains have been discovered. Some tombs were clearly intended for burials, but at others the evidence is not so convincing. They may have had another purpose that we cannot yet fully understand.

In Northern Ireland alone there are records of 639 megalithic tomb sites. In the whole of Ireland there are over 1,500 known megalithic tombs (for convenience in this book they are also called megalithic monuments). There are four main types of tombs discussed in this book, but not all of the sites found in Northern Ireland can be neatly classified as one type or another. There are regional variations in the kinds of tombs and their distribution, and these are usually the subject of lots of archaeological debate.

Megalithic tombs are also found in Great Britain, and there are significant regional

Beaghmore Stone Circles, County Tyrone

variations there too. The tombs found in Britain and Ireland are part of wider distributions along the Atlantic coasts of Europe and North Africa, from Scandinavia in the north, to Morocco in the south.

Northern Ireland is sometimes seen as being on the edge of European development. But it is right at the centre of activity as far as megalithic tombs are concerned. Northern Ireland is in fact one of the best places in the world to see megalithic monuments – and increasing numbers of people want to get out and see this marvellous part of our heritage.

The NIEA encourages everyone to get out and about to see our megalithic tombs. Quite a few are almost intact, but it is also worth bearing in mind that many have been damaged in the past, or have not yet been fully exposed. Sometimes there will be nothing more than a collection of large stones, with no obvious shape or function. Gorse or heather bushes might make it hard to see a stone never mind a tomb: the monument might only be visible on close inspection. Where this is the case, the present-day remains are usually the last surviving pieces of a much larger monument. The missing portions of the site might have been lost or removed over centuries of exposure to weather, people and animals.

More often than not the locations of these monuments are still spectacular. There will always be an opportunity to see or to imagine what was there in ancient times and to discover something fascinating. Creggandevesky Court Tomb was all but hidden under a thick layer of peat bog

Guardians of our built heritage

Ancient and historic monuments, buildings and landscapes are referred to collectively as our 'built heritage'. Many have special protection that will help ensure they survive into the future. The Northern Ireland Environment Agency (NIEA) manages over 190 historic monuments in its care. These monuments are open to the public, and most can be visited free of charge. The NIEA works closely with the owners of historic monuments to help keep the sites safe. The NIEA also has special responsibility in Northern Ireland for heritage protection, such as the reporting of archaeological discoveries including treasure.

in County Tyrone. Only a few stones poked up above the ground surface. Archaeological excavation and recording revealed one of the most impressive and well preserved monuments of its type in Northern Ireland. It has been carefully conserved and is now open to the public. Even a short visit will give you a glimpse of its former glory.

Shrouds of myth and legend

Without modern knowledge and scientific study it would be hard for us to understand

Creggandevesky Court Tomb, County Tyrone

megalithic tombs – remember, even 2,000 years ago these monuments were already ancient. It is no surprise that people in the past had many beliefs, myths, folk stories and legends around these mysterious sites, just as they did for many other historic sites throughout Ireland. Ireland's reputation as a land of myth and legend is among the richest in the world.

Archaeologists think that many stories about megaliths are often based on myths and legends that developed in the Iron Age, early Medieval and Viking periods, but some of the stories could be much older. These stories are seen in the names of some tombs. There

are tombs with names like 'The Hag's Chair', 'King's Ring', 'Diarmuid and Gráinne's Bed', or the 'Stone House'. The most common names for megalithic tombs are 'the Druid's Altar' or the 'Giant's Grave'.

Some tombs are associated with the great mythological heroes of Irish society or the religious rites of the Celts and earlier peoples. The story of Diarmuid and Gráinne, Ireland's most tragic lovers, is one of the most popular. It is an early medieval legend telling of Gráinne, the young and beautiful daughter of Cormac mac Airt, High King of Ireland. She was to be married to an aging Fionn mac Cumhaill (Finn McCool), but

Ballywholan Portal Tomb, County Tyrone

at the last minute she eloped with one of Fionn's young warriors named Diarmuid O' Duibhne. As a result Fionn and his band of warriors endlessly pursued the two lovers around Ireland, until Diarmuid finally met his death at the hands of Fionn. Gráinne died of a broken heart. According to legend, as they fled from Fionn Mac Cumhaill, the couple slept in secret places all over Ireland. Many places still bear the name 'Diarmuid and Gráinne's Bed'.

When Christianity arrived in Ireland it began to mix with, adopt and influence the older traditions and beliefs about the ancient sites. Today there are still strong associations with religious figures, including the best

known of them all – St Patrick. For example, Ballywholan Portal Tomb in County Tyrone has a local name of 'Carnfadrick' (Patrick's Cairn) because – according to tradition – the saint is said to have travelled by it on the way to visiting a friend.

Another fabulous tale left to us from the past involves the megalithic tomb on the summit of Slieve Gullion in County Armagh. There is a tomb on Slieve Gullion known locally as 'Calliagh Berra's House'. Calliagh Berra was a sort of evil witch who is said to have enticed the mighty Fionn Mac Cumhaill into the 'house' on the summit. From there she took him deep into the earth. When he came back out of the tomb he had become an emaciated old man, and it took years before he managed to fully regain his strength.

Strange and wonderful tales involving megalithic tombs and other prehistoric sites are found all over Northern Ireland. For instance the Slaghtaverty burial cairn near Coleraine, County Londonderry, is the reputed burial site of an infamous dwarf who terrorised local people, and enchanted women with his magical powers and the music he played on his harp.

Tomb detectives

Whatever stories and place names have evolved for megalithic tombs, they have always been identified with someone or something special from the past. This added mystery to the tombs, and these traditions almost certainly helped to protect many of the sites from human interference. However, it has also attracted the inquisitive.

During the nineteenth century antiquarians dug into many megalithic monuments in a bid to discover their secrets. Sometimes their work was very crude and it destroyed much of the material encountered in the process. However, these antiquarians regularly found that someone had already beaten them to it at some time in the distant past. Many tombs were found to be already badly damaged, probably by treasure hunters.

Clontygora Court Tomb, County Armagh

Early pioneers

What we know about Northern Ireland's megalithic tombs today is largely due to the pioneering work of archaeologists from yesteryear.

Estyn Evans

Professor Estyn Evans (1905-1989), independent lecturer and later Professor of Geography at Queen's University, was a pioneer of heritage studies and one of the first to carry out systematic excavations in Northern Ireland.

Oliver Davies

Oliver Davies (1905-1986) was a lecturer in classical archaeology at Queen's University and pioneered excavations at megalithic monuments in Northern Ireland, along with Estyn Evans. They published many excavation reports in the Third Edition of the Ulster Journal of Archaeology, which began in 1938. In 1950, the Ministry of Finance established the Archaeological Survey of Northern Ireland, with Pat Collins and Dudley Waterman continuing the work of Evans and Davies.

Dudley Waterman

Dudley Waterman (1918-1979) directed his initial efforts to County Down, with An Archaeological Survey of County Down published in 1966. He also excavated and published on many megalithic tombs in Northern Ireland, but is perhaps best known for his work at Navan Fort in County Armagh.

Pat Collins

Alfred Edward Patrick, or 'Pat' Collins (1921-1991) as he was known, was also very active in the excavation and publishing of many of the prehistoric sites in Northern Ireland, with over 40 articles and notes published in the Ulster Journal of Archaeology alone since 1950. The meticulous work of archaeologists such as Waterman and Collins has greatly enhanced our understanding of megalithic tombs in general.

It was not until the twentieth century that a more scientific study was made of these monuments in Northern Ireland. This was led by pioneering archaeologists such as Oliver Davies, Estyn Evans, Pat Collins and Dudley Waterman. Their work still informs the debate about the origin and use of these monuments.

It is the archaeologist's job to examine megalithic tombs and other ancient sites and objects to learn about them and to add to our constantly growing understanding of the peoples of the past. The dilemma for the profession has always been that more evidence about the people who constructed the tombs probably lies below ground than above it. Many sites are hidden below our feet.

In finding out about tombs, modern archaeologists have many different techniques at their disposal, including excavation. It is rare that archaeologists get the opportunity to excavate these megalithic tomb sites: many have special protection, and through negotiation with landowners and developers most can be protected for

the future. But they still attract attention, and from time to time we get the chance to look a little deeper.

From the excavations that have happened in the past it is clear that some features are common to many megalithic tombs. These are things like chambers or galleries, defined by large upright stones or slabs called orthostats.

Other tombs displayed features such as a single huge stone at the top of the monument, supported by two or more vertical stone pillars, or arrangements of stones connected to the main galleries.

Wateresk Portal Tomb, County Down

Excavation practice

Excavation is a destructive process. It is an excellent way to find out about the past, but the techniques of digging a site means that it is basically taken apart. Once this happens it cannot fully be put back together again. The decision to excavate a site is usually the second option: the first option is to try to preserve it for the future. Archaeological techniques are improving all the time, and future generations might be able to find out much more about the sites than we can – provided the sites survive into the future.

Sometimes an excavation is necessary because a site has been damaged or is under threat. Sometimes a portion of a site is excavated for research, and the dig is planned to try to find out as much as possible from a sample of the site.

During an excavation archaeologists use a method known as 'relative dating'. This relies on the idea that the most modern layer is usually at the top, the ground surface. Older layers are encountered as the excavator digs downwards into the ground. Artefacts found in these layers can be used to date the site. Techniques vary by the type of site, but all methods of archaeological excavation require great skill and patience.

Excavations are followed by what is usually a 'hidden' phase of post-excavation work. This is when artefacts are analysed, classified, dated and the results published. Research excavations may last months or even years. Most digs are nowadays short-term excavations before new construction work. Over the past ten years there has been a big increase in the number of excavations in Northern Ireland, with lots of new sites being uncovered.

In Northern Ireland all digs to search for archaeological material must be specially licensed and are usually led by a professional archaeologist.

These features allowed archaeologists to categorise the monuments into the small number of basic types. The different types are named after the most distinctive features at each site, although every tomb seems to be unique in its own way.

Gradually, archaeologists have shed much light on the mysteries and myths about our megalithic tombs. But there is still much to learn. For instance many monuments today still do not fit easily into the different categories currently in use. Their 'unclassified' description means that some of the most basic information about the sites has not yet been discovered, and we simply do not know what is inside them.

There are still many mysteries about these sites. How did they move the stones? Why

Clontygora Court Tomb, County Armagh

Academic archaeology

The academic study of archaeology in Ulster began in 1909, when Queen's University established a department of archaeology, but this fell victim to wartime cuts and it was not re-established until 1948. Today, archaeology is studied at the School of Geography, Archaeology and Palaeoecology and the university is a world leader in the study of several archaeological technologies, including radiocarbon dating, dendrochronology and palaeoecology. Queen's is also home to the Centre for Archaeological Fieldwork, which excavates and surveys on behalf of the NIEA in addition to its academic functions. At the University of Ulster, the Centre for Maritime Archaeology has a similar role, but specialises in marine and coastal archaeology.

Commercial archaeology

Commercial archaeological companies emerged during the 1990s to meet the need for increased archaeological monitoring and excavation at public and private sector developments. Commercial archaeologists spend much of their time 'rescuing' archaeology at sites that are about to be built upon. If the archaeological remains cannot be protected in the ground, it has to be excavated and recorded. Commercial archaeological companies' work is largely funded by developers in the private sector, and this work is regulated by the NIEA.

Craigs Passage Tomb, County Antrim

did they choose these locations? Had anything happened at the site before the tomb was built? What happened afterwards?

Today, professional and amateur archaeologists in Northern Ireland carry on the work of their forbears. The archaeological profession has made huge developments over the past 60 years. This is particularly the case for new and developing scientific techniques.

Even though earlier antiquarians were often privileged people, and modern archaeology makes use of lots of scientific techniques, the tombs themselves can be enjoyed by everyone.

Who built them and when?

From the radiocarbon dating evidence obtained so far, archaeologists can tell that

Archaeology today

Most archaeology is practised by professionals in government bodies, planning departments and field archaeology units, museums and universities. But you can get involved too. If you are fascinated by the past and have an urge to learn and discover more, why not join your local archaeological society to find out what interesting sites are near to you?

The principal archaeological society in Northern Ireland is the Ulster Archaeological Society, founded in 1853. New members are always welcome and details of their activities can be found at http://uas.society.qub.ac.uk. Details of many local historical societies can also be obtained from the Foundation for Ulster Local Studies at http://www.fuls.org.uk.

construction of the tombs began around 6,000 years ago, at around 4000 BC. This means that it was Neolithic people, the first farmers, who built our earliest megalithic monuments. Radiocarbon dating is a scientific technique used to find out the age of substances like wood and bone, and is a key part of the archaeological study of megalithic tombs.

Neolithic people lived within the time period archaeologists and historians call prehistory – the period before humans started to write down what was happening in society. To put the people who built the megalithic monuments in context, the last ice age in Ireland ended around 13,000 years ago and one of the earliest human dwelling sites so far discovered in Ireland, Mount Sandel near Coleraine, dates from around 9,000 years ago (7000 BC).

Radiocarbon dating

An American scientist, Willard Libby, developed the first radiocarbon dating technique in the late 1940s. The technique determines the age of a sample of organic material (charred wood, plant roots, cloth etc). Radiocarbon is present in plant material and eventually makes its way into all living organisms, where it remains until the death of the organism, and then it begins to decay at a steady rate. By measuring the amount of radiocarbon remaining in a sample, scientists can estimate the period of time that has passed since the organism died. Queen's University, Belfast is at the forefront of this technology.

A view from the passage tomb at the Giant's Ring, County Down

Reconstruction drawing of a Mesolithic camp site

Archaeologists divide prehistory into different chunks of time to make it easier to describe the course of human activity here. For example, the earliest settlers in Ireland did not use metal, and most of the artefacts that have been discovered are made of stone. So this period is referred to as the Stone Age. The Stone Age then gets sub-divided into the old, middle and new Stone Age – in archaeological terms, the Palaeolithic, Mesolithic and Neolithic periods. The differences between each period are largely based on the types of artefacts found.

The 'old' Stone Age (the Palaeolithic period) refers to all human activity up to about 10,000 years ago (8000 BC). Some flint tools

have been found in Ireland that might belong to this period, but so far we do not have any identified Palaeolithic sites.

The 'middle' Stone Age (the Mesolithic period) lasted from about 10,000–6,000 years ago (8000–4000 BC) and there is good evidence that it was during this period that hunter-gatherer peoples first came to Ireland.

The 'new' Stone Age (the Neolithic period) began about 6,000 years ago (4000 BC) and lasted until around 4,500 years ago (2500 BC).

It was in the Neolithic period that farming was introduced to Ireland, the nomadic

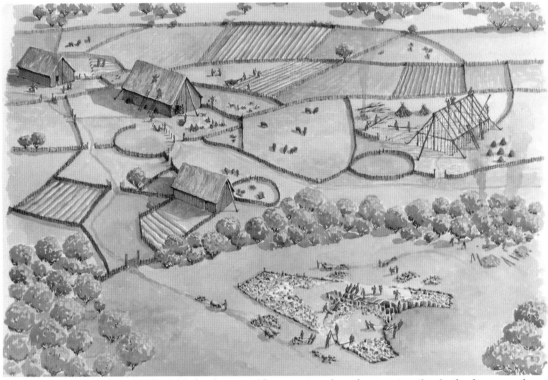

Reconstruction drawing of a Neolithic landscape with a court tomb under construction in the foreground

hunter-gathering way of life came to an end, and the Neolithic peoples began to construct megalithic tombs.

The remainder of prehistory stretches from the Neolithic into the Bronze Age and the Iron Age. In the Bronze Age, metalworking, first with copper and gold, later with bronze, was introduced to Ireland. It started around 4,500 years ago (2500 BC) and continued until about 2,300 years ago (300 BC), when objects made of iron were first introduced. From about 1,600 years ago (the date often given is AD 430), occasional written evidence of human life begins, usually related to the early Christian church. So this point in time marks the transition from the prehistoric to the historic periods.

Even without historical documents it is still possible to build up a picture of what prehistoric people were like and what it was like to live in prehistoric times. To do this, archaeologists can use various techniques, including information and records from excavations and the scientific study of past environments.

For example, in a typical pollen record taken from a bog or lake in Northern Ireland, we can see how the natural environment was changed. Grasslands eventually gave way to forests after the Ice Age. When the first people arrived in Ireland they would have been faced with thick forests of mainly pine and hazel. This meant life 10,000 years ago was probably restricted to coastal and river areas.

Ancient ecology, pollen and animals

Archaeologists can build a picture of environmental change over considerable periods of time using palaeoecology, a science that studies fossil plants' and animals' relationship to their environment, and palynology, the study of contemporary and fossil pollen.

Palynologists have found that trees and other plants produce vast quantities of pollen. Some pollen grains can survive for thousands of years. When pollen is blown on to the surface of a lake, it settles to the bottom and is eventually covered by later layers of silt. If a sample of silt can be taken and the trapped pollen grains examined, the species of plants that were growing nearby can be identified. Pollen records can also be radiocarbon dated, providing a dated sequence of events. This can then be used to help in the study of our ancestors.

The study of fossil animal bones also tells us about the environment of the past. For example, we know that many of the domesticated species present in Northern Ireland today, including cattle, sheep and goats, were not present in Ireland during the Mesolithic period. We can conclude that early Neolithic immigrants initially imported these species as live cargo, and that these animals were central to their way of life.

In these times archaeologists think that people moved from area to area through the year. They hunted animals, gathered fruit, seeds and nuts as the seasons allowed. They probably lived in small huts like those

A Mesolithic hut site under excavation at Mount Sandel, Coleraine, County Londonderry

discovered at Mount Sandel. Studies of the remains of animals from this and other sites tell us that the middle Stone Age diet included wild pigs, salmon, trout and eels. Mesolithic people also hunted wild birds, including pigeon, duck and grouse.

The pollen analysis shows that this Mesolithic hunter-gatherer way of life continued in Ireland until about 6,000 years ago (4000 BC), the beginning of the Neolithic period. After this time there was a marked decline in tree pollen and a rise in cereal pollen, suggesting that people were clearing large areas of forest to plant crops.

Tree pollen accounted for as much as 80 or 90% of the total pollen 6,000 years ago. By 1,000 years ago this had fallen to just 30%:

Neolithic arrowheads from Carrowreagh, Dundonald

the trees were disappearing fast. Variations in pollen types throughout new Stone Age times confirm the kind of farming activity and Neolithic society.

As the Neolithic population increased they cleared more and more forests. Communication between families and small groups would have been made easier, allowing larger social groups to develop. Archaeologists have suggested that this provided the social conditions for the construction of megalithic monuments.

Their technology was wood, stone and animal bones – used to make picks, shovels, pins and personal ornaments. Most of the tools that survive are stone, particularly flint, but they also used basalt, mudstone and shale. They also made earthenware pots for cooking and for storing food. There is evidence they used wood to construct their dwellings and to make other household items.

A large number of flint tools such as scrapers have been found at tombs, indicating that animal skins were being processed routinely. It is likely these formed a main part of the Neolithic wardrobe.

Studies of Neolithic people's bones reveal that the majority did not live to be older than 35. There also appears to have been a high infant mortality rate and diseases such as arthritis were common.

Evidence of the daily life of the Neolithic people remains scant, but it seems likely that most of their time and effort was devoted to growing crops and tending to animals.

Neolithic burials, Millin Bay, County Down

Despite being occupied with this they managed to build hundreds of megalithic tombs. The monuments were clearly very important to people at that time.

The structures they left behind, the artefacts found in and around the tombs, the tombs' internal layout, their positioning and location in the landscape, and the thousands of years of history they represent provide a great treasure full of opportunities for appreciation, interpretation and study – a megalithic legacy for all to enjoy.

What did they leave behind?

The Neolithic people left behind at least 639 megalithic tombs in Northern Ireland. Of these, 33 are 'passage' tombs, 126 are 'court' tombs, 53 are 'portal' tombs, and 60 are 'wedge' tombs. A further 367 (57%) cannot be classified at present.

One of the most interesting legacies from these monuments is human remains. Where human remains are found, archaeologists have discovered that the remains usually represent only a few individuals at each tomb. For example, in court tombs the remains of only two or three people are usually found, although there are a few notable exceptions (34 individuals were found at a tomb in Audleystown, County Down and 21 at Creggandevesky, County Tyrone). Clearly not everyone in Neolithic society was being buried in megalithic tombs. Some sort of selection process must have been used to decide whose remains would be placed inside these tombs.

Museums

Museums throughout Ireland and further afield hold many of the items recovered from archaeological excavations throughout Northern Ireland. At the Ulster Museum at Stranmillis Road, Belfast, there are substantial collections of Neolithic material, including the Malone Hoard of nineteen porcellanite axe heads. Museum collections have often been initiated or enhanced by donations from private collections, such as that of Canon John Grainger from Broughshane in County Antrim.

Archaeologists meticulously record everything they find, from the stones used in construction, to the smallest artefacts and even the nature of the soils found inside the tombs. It has been found that the acidic soil widespread in Northern Ireland is not good for preserving human bones. But through detecting increased levels of chemicals such as phosphates archaeologists can still indicate that bone material was once present.

Despite the acidic soils, sometimes bone does survive in megalithic tombs. Sometimes bones were put into the burial chambers. Other human remains include cremations, and burnt bone fragments survive quite well. The way the bones are deposited in the tombs indicates that there were special rituals involved. The evidence suggests that not all of the body was put into the tombs,

Ballykeel Portal Tomb, County Armagh

as in modern cemeteries, but it clearly indicates that the monuments had a special association with the dead.

The radiocarbon dates from some of the bones and charcoal found at tomb excavations confirm that most of the tombs were constructed during the Neolithic period. Some were re-used later, especially in the early Bronze Age. These dates also show that several tomb types – portal, court and passage – were being used at the same time. This means that it is unlikely one type gave way to another over time.

At various sites archaeologists have found many items associated with daily life: tools, personal ornaments and pottery fragments (archaeologists call pottery fragments

'sherds'). Collectively, these artefacts have become known as 'grave goods'. They give us further insights into the sort of things that were used by Neolithic people.

Some items, such as polished stone beads, were intended for personal adornment. Other finds, such as javelin heads and arrowheads were clearly weapons. Other flint items, such as blades, hollow scrapers and end scrapers, would have been used for processing animal skins. They probably represent the sort of tools that Neolithic people would have used on a daily basis.

Items made of stone and pottery will survive almost indefinitely. But more perishable materials such as wood and animal skins decay and leave little or no trace. So there

Ballykeel Portal Tomb, County Armagh

The world of Neolithic pottery

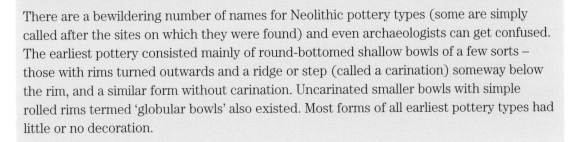

Prehistoric pottery was handmade from coils of clay much like the way children are still taught in primary school today. It was then baked hard in bonfires. The earliest northern Irish pottery is very similar to pottery found at the same time elsewhere in the western British Isles. This originally led archaeologists to give it the name 'Western Neolithic'. The name has been replaced by the new term of 'traditional carinated bowl'.

There are a bewildering number of names for Neolithic pottery types (some are simply called after the sites on which they were found) and even archaeologists can get confused. The earliest pottery consisted mainly of round-bottomed shallow bowls of a few sorts – those with rims turned outwards and a ridge or step (called a carination) someway below the rim, and a similar form without carination. Uncarinated smaller bowls with simple rolled rims termed 'globular bowls' also existed. Most forms of all earliest pottery types had little or no decoration.

Pottery became more varied during the middle and later Neolithic periods. Undecorated and carinated types tended to be lesser in number.

As time passed, regional styles emerged along with different forms for domestic, ceremonial and burial activities. By the beginning of the early Bronze Age some pottery styles remained plain but were increasingly accompanied by highly decorated pots called 'Beakers' – a style of ceramics adopted from the continent, possibly associated with the consumption of alcohol and sometimes found in wedge tomb burials.

may once have been a much greater variety of grave goods in our megalithic tombs. In addition, items that were placed in the tombs at first may have been pushed to one side or removed to make room for additional deposits. The remains might have been cleared out from time to time. Or they may simply have been stolen or scattered by later grave robbers or treasure hunters. What we are left with today may only represent the result of many years of disturbance.

It is very common to find pottery in megalithic tombs, usually as sherds, but sometimes there are enough pieces to allow the reconstruction of the original item. At an excavation of a court tomb at Annaghmare in County Armagh, archaeologists found sherds of several different undecorated early Neolithic pots. At another excavation at Ballykeel Portal Tomb, County Armagh, decorated bowls known as 'carinated bowls' were found.

The latest tomb finds in Northern Ireland

The most recent finds from a megalithic tomb in Northern Ireland came to light in 2010 in County Londonderry as archaeologists began the excavation of a portal tomb for the first time in 45 years.

The NIEA and the Centre for Archaeological Fieldwork at Queen's University began the excavation at Tirnony Portal Tomb after it had begun to collapse. Weather had caused cracking in some of the chamber stones supporting the capstone. The NIEA intended to restore the 5,000–6,000 year-old tomb but as the restoration may have damaged important archaeological material the excavation took place first – providing a rare opportunity to investigate a tomb with modern techniques.

The finds included six different pottery vessels, at least five of which have been confirmed as early Neolithic, and two impressive flint knives, also Neolithic. A blue glass bead of Iron Age or early Medieval date was also found.

Only a very few, and very small pieces of bone were found in the tomb, suggesting that most of the human remains, presumably placed within the tomb, have decayed. The pottery and flint knives may have been placed into the tomb during funerary rituals. It is possible that the blue glass bead was placed in the tomb during a later burial, as archaeologists have found that these tombs continued to be used for burials long after they were first constructed, but it is more likely that the bead was placed in the tomb in a non-funerary ritual.

Where did they build them?

Megalithic tombs are found across Ireland, although distribution patterns vary greatly for each type. Many of the concentrations are found in the north and west of the island, but many have been destroyed in the past and it is very difficult to be precise about the total number and locations of megalithic tombs that were actually constructed.

Portal tombs and court tombs are generally located in the northern part of Ireland, with additional clusters of portal tombs in counties Clare, Waterford and in the south of County Kilkenny.

You will find passage tombs in all parts of Ireland except the very south-west. There are notable clusters of passage tombs, in what are called 'passage tomb cemeteries'. These are found in the Boyne Valley and at Carrowmore and Carrowkeel in County Sligo. There are smaller clusters of passage tombs in north Antrim and at Sess Kilgreen near Ballygawley in County Tyrone.

Sess Kilgreen Neolithic art, County Tyrone

Wedge tombs are a feature of the western side of Ireland, although they are also found in County Antrim. No wedge tombs have yet been found in counties Armagh and Down.

More than half of the sites do not easily fit into any of the main categories of tomb.

There are two main reasons for this. First, many of the early documentary references to tombs that have since been destroyed do not have enough detail to be sure what type of tombs they refer to. Secondly, many surviving tombs have not been excavated, and not enough features are visible to make a definite classification.

County	Megalithic tomb (unclassified)	Court tomb	Portal tomb	Passage tomb	Wedge tomb	Total
Antrim	138	26	6	13	12	195
Armagh	20	10	6	6	0	42
Down	23	16	10	3	0	52
Fermanagh	40	26	2	2	11	81
Londonderry	91	13	6	1	13	124
Tyrone	55	35	23	8	24	145
Total	367	126	53	33	60	639

Giant's Ring, Ballynahatty, County Down

It must also be remembered that there are probably many 'new' megalithic tombs that have not yet been recorded. They might survive under areas of blanket bog, just like the tomb at Creggandevesky.

Why did they build them?

Over the last 60 years or so, with systematic archaeological excavations and the application of scientific techniques, some of the secrets of Northern Ireland's megalithic tombs have been revealed. The shape, size, dates, locations, number and finds associated with tombs provide intriguing insights into the life and death of our early ancestors.

However, there is still much to learn about when, how and why our prehistoric ancestors constructed their fascinating megalithic tombs.

Much study, thought and debate about the chronological sequence of the megalithic tombs has taken place. This work is complicated because it seems successive generations of our ancestors often used the existing tombs more than once. They may have cleared out or moved older remains to make room for their own dead.

The size and shape of megalithic tombs reveals some information about the structure itself and possibly those who constructed it. For example, we could presume that larger or more sophisticated groups built the larger and more complex monuments, and that they perhaps represent the burial of wealthy or powerful people.

We also know that the tradition of building new megalithic tombs died out around the end of the Neolithic period. From the middle of the Bronze Age until the end of the prehistoric period in Ireland, burials tended to be within stone or earth mounds, or in underground cists or pits, often leaving very little trace on the surface.

Megalithic tombs must have held a special place in early societies. They required significant expenditures of time and labour, along with specialist skills in their location and construction. Clearly the megalithic tomb-builders of Northern Ireland intended their monuments to last, unlike their homes of timber or wattle, which left no lasting mark in the landscape.

There is evidence from the spectacular Giant's Ring site near Belfast that Neolithic people had the ability to come together in larger groups and move enormous amounts of heavy materials over great distances. The scale of the imposing Giant's Ring earthwork, some 200m in diameter and today still standing 4m high, suggests that there were sophisticated organising skills in use. This might have involved slave labour, but it is equally possible that building these monuments was a shared, communal activity. What is clear, however, is that large amounts of food and supplies and a great number of workers were needed over long periods of time to complete such projects.

Prehistoric burial practices

New research on excavated prehistoric remains in Ireland suggests that cremation was the predominant burial practice during the Neolithic and Bronze Age. Disarticulation (the burial of selected bones from a body that had been de-fleshed elsewhere) was predominantly a feature of Neolithic society and it is not surprising that disarticulated bones are often found inside megalithic tombs. It has also been found that prehistoric people had very low levels of dental disease, but many suffered from degenerative joint disease and osteoarthritis in their shoulders and necks, suggesting they routinely carried heavy loads, possibly on their heads.

Close to the Giant's Ring, Barrie Hartwell of Queen's University discovered an extensive complex of timber posts in 1989. Crop marks in fields around the monument were seen on photographs taken from an aircraft. These marks are patterns in the vegetation of the fields that reveal the presence of archaeological features underneath the

Tirnony Portal Tomb, County Londonderry

surface. Sometimes they can be seen from the air.

Part of the site was later excavated and the dig revealed hundreds of post-holes that formed circles and alignments. Some of the post-holes were large enough to hold oak posts with a diameter of 1.5m and the posts would have weighed an incredible 10 tonnes.

What was the huge structure for? Why did the Neolithic people build it? The answer is that no-one really knows. Clues can be picked up from the artefacts found at the sites and the setting of the monuments in the surrounding landscapes. Ultimately though, we can only speculate as to its function.

Perhaps because of their high visibility, megalithic tombs attracted the attention of treasure hunters and antiquarians for many hundreds of years. Their activities might have destroyed much of the fragile evidence of Neolithic burials.

Thankfully, however, our prehistoric monuments now have statutory protection from treasure seekers. Research continues into monuments that have already been excavated. The discovery of new ones during development work is an ongoing process, constantly adding to our understanding.

Northern Ireland's megalithic tombs are a wonderfully visual – yet enigmatic – legacy from a time when human beings began to

Geophysics

Archaeologists can use a number of techniques to discover the location of archaeological features without disturbing the site. Geophysical surveys – sometimes shortened to 'geophys' – include ground-penetrating radar that captures images of sub-surface structures, changes in materials, voids and cracks. Other geophysical methods include magnetic susceptibility (this identifies changes in the magnetism of soils caused by heating) and resistivity (identifies changes in the electrical conductivity of soils) that can point to the presence of ditches, pits and walls even when there is nothing to be seen on the surface. In the future, new scientific techniques will probably become available that can reveal even more about ancient sites without the need for excavation.

make a lasting mark on the landscape. The tantalising glimpses we get from the distant past have, for many years, inspired an interest in learning about these monuments and the people who created them.

How did they move the massive stones?

One of the most intriguing secrets held by megalithic tombs surrounds how the Neolithic people managed to build them with only basic tools and equipment. The enormous capstone of Browneshill Portal Tomb in County Carlow weighs in at around 150 tonnes (equivalent to the weight of about 12 double-decker buses) and is thought to be the heaviest in Europe. How did Neolithic people move these huge boulders, let alone lift them into position over the supporting uprights? The answer remains the subject of much debate.

Many of the larger stones used in tomb construction were probably already present on or near the site. The retreating glaciers of the last ice age left behind many huge stones on the Irish landscape. These stones, often known as glacial erratics, are large pieces of rock that were carried along in glaciers, and then dropped on top of the landscape as the ice melted. But there is also evidence that other stones were deliberately quarried out of nearby rock formations and then dragged to the tomb construction site.

One possibility for tomb construction is that the Neolithic people first, through lots of physical effort, manhandled the uprights into position. They then built an earth or stone ramp up around them. Once this was done, they dragged the capstones up the slope. After the capstone was in place, they removed the earth or stone ramp.

This sounds a lot easier than it actually must have been, when we think of the effort required to move even a small boulder. But several experiments have been carried out to see if such construction methods could have worked. They have generally proved successful.

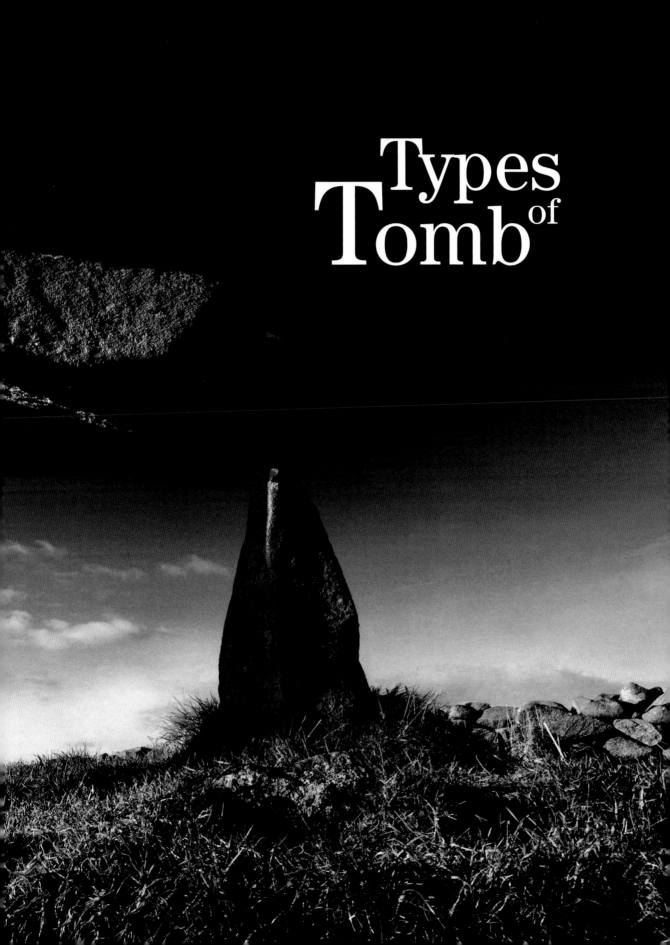

Types of Tomb

Portal tombs

Portal tombs are perhaps the most dramatic of Northern Ireland's megalithic tombs, as the picturesque Legananny Portal Tomb in County Down illustrates. The stones used combine to give the appearance of a doorway, or portal, usually very large, and their huge capstones make them among the most photographed and publicised of all megalithic monuments.

Portal tomb capstones are usually supported by upright stone slabs. One capstone at Kilfeaghan, County Down, weighs in at around 35 tonnes – the weight of about three double-decker buses. The capstones are often balanced precariously on the tips of the orthostats. A number have slipped off at some time in the past; others were deliberately removed. One example at Drumderg in County Londonderry was used to make a millstone.

Kilfeaghan Portal Tomb, County Down

Portal tombs have been given names like 'dolmen', or 'portal dolmen' and many have colourful local names, such as the 'Druid's Altar' (Ballylumford, County Antrim), 'Giant's Grave' (Glengesh, County Fermanagh), or 'Diarmuid and Gráinne's Bed' (Murnells, County Tyrone). A few have even acquired multiple names. At Goward, County Down, the locals refer to 'Goward Dolmen', 'Cloghmore Cromlech', 'Pat Kearney's Big Stone' and 'Finn's Fingerstones'.

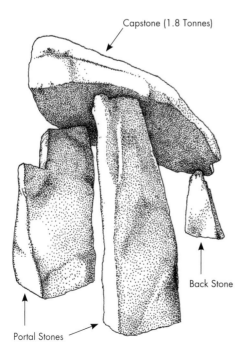
Capstone (1.8 Tonnes)
Back Stone
Portal Stones

Murnells Portal Tomb, County Tyrone

Legananny Portal Tomb, County Down
Previous spread: Ballykeel Portal Tomb, County Armagh

Despite the number of portal tombs present in Northern Ireland, only eight have ever been excavated. Two, at Greengraves in County Down and Ballywholan in County Tyrone, were the subject of antiquarian attention in 1830 and 1897 respectively, but detailed records were not kept of the findings. The results of the most recent dig at Tirnony in County Londonderry are still being analysed.

The only portal tombs excavated scientifically have been:
- Clonlum, County Armagh, by Oliver Davies and Estyn Evans in 1935
- Ballyrenan, County Tyrone, by Oliver Davies in 1936
- Ticloy, County Antrim, by Davies and Watson in 1942
- Kilfeaghan, County Down, by Pat Collins in 1959
- Ballykeel, County Armagh, by Pat Collins in 1965
- Tirnony, County Londonderry, by Mc Sparron, Logue and Williams in 2010-11

Archaeologists depend on the information from these few excavations for much of our knowledge about the portal tombs of Northern Ireland. However, we can refer to others in Ireland and further afield to gain a wider understanding about these monuments. For example, a major analysis of all known portal tombs in Britain and

Greengraves Portal Tomb, County Down

Ticloy Portal Tomb, County Antrim

Ireland, completed at Queen's University in 2008, has added significantly to our knowledge of these monuments.

Shape and form

In the Republic of Ireland during the 1940s, a survey of all known megalithic tombs in Ireland was begun and the first volume was published in 1961. In it, Ruaidhrí de Valera and Seán Ó Nualláin provided a definition of the shape and form of a portal tomb. It could almost be used as a guide for anyone wanting to build such a structure today. It reads:

"The principal characteristics of portal tombs are, a single chamber of rectilinear design, usually narrowing towards the rear, having an entry between two tall portal stones set inside the line of sidestones and covered by a capstone often of enormous size, poised high above the entrance and sloping down towards the rear of the chamber. The capstone is frequently raised clear of

the sidestones and rests on the portal stone and backstone. Usually each side and the back are formed of single slabs. Frequently beneath the great capstone is a smaller cover resting on the sides and backstone and in this case the rear end of the principal cap rests on the second cover rather than on the backstone. Between the portals a slab closing the entrance is present in many sites, often reaching full height, but sometimes only three-quarters or half the height of the portal jambs. Occasionally, in place of the high slab a sill is found, while in many instances no evidence of closure, partial or full, appears. In a few examples high stones flanking the entrance are present. A bias towards placing the entrance eastwards is present in portal tombs. The mound shape is rarely clearly defined but both long and round forms are attested."

Modern archaeologists still observe these general rules of description, though it has to be said that the prehistoric tomb builders did not stick rigidly to them – many sites have their own unique features.

Measurements taken on 35 surviving portal tomb capstones in Northern Ireland have found that they vary in volume from 0.83m^3 to 24m^3. The average is around 6m^3, comparable with other portal tombs throughout Ireland, Wales and Cornwall.

The weight of the stones varies from one rock type to another, but it has been estimated that portal tomb capstones in Northern Ireland vary from the relatively modest 2.2 tonnes of Cloghfin in County

Goward Portal Tomb, County Down

Tyrone to the massive 50 tonnes of granite at Goward in County Down – equivalent to the weight of four double-decker buses.

Portal tombs were normally constructed from the local rock type, often moved only a few metres into position. However, where available, rocks with quartz veins – a shiny mineral that glints in sunlight – were often used.

Many portal tombs could have been erected by an extended family, but the larger capstones would have required a social organisation beyond the family group. So, the size of the capstone chosen may have had some relationship with the numbers and ability of people available to move it into position.

In comparison with other megalithic tomb types, portal tombs are relatively simple, suggesting that these monuments were early attempts in megalithic tomb-building. Some sites contain a pair of tombs, but most of the portal tombs in Northern Ireland are found as single monuments. Very few have surviving evidence of a covering cairn.

Location and positioning

A recent survey of Northern Ireland prehistoric burial sites identified a total of 53 known portal tombs, with a further 10 possible sites. The larger number can only be confirmed through excavation, but the 53 known examples alone represent almost 30% of the total for the whole of Ireland.

In Ireland, the number of known portal tombs is estimated at between 174 and 184. Of the 53 known portal tombs in Northern Ireland, 23 are situated in County Tyrone.

Research suggests that portal tomb builders followed strict ideas about where they were to be built in the landscape. The vast majority of portal tombs are beside streams, and more often than not they face upstream, towards the source of the water.

Portal tombs are also found along the sides of drumlins, in smaller river valleys and close to the sea, and are always positioned below the highest point in the area. Evidence also suggests that the portal tomb builders

County	Portal tombs	Possible portal tombs
Antrim	6	0
Armagh	6	0
Down	10	3
Fermanagh	2	1
Londonderry	6	1
Tyrone	23	2
Total	**53**	**7**

preferred a south facing slope, with the portal – the entrance to the tomb-facing to the east. Most are situated at lower altitudes, between 5m and 150m above sea level. None are found at altitudes higher than 330m.

Some portal tombs, such as Tirnony near Maghera in County Londonderry, are in

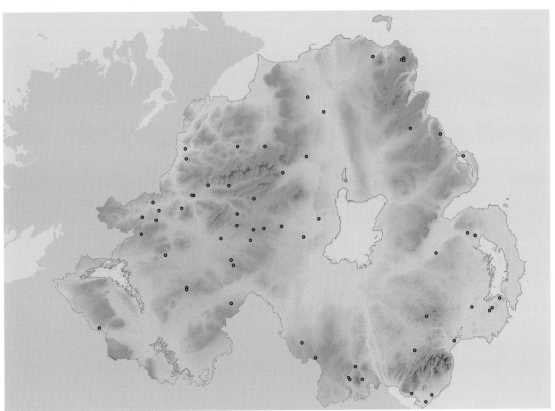

Distribution map of portal tombs in Northern Ireland

Site	Finds
Ballykeel, County Armagh	6 plain carinated vessels
	Small javelin head
	3 decorated carinated bowls
	300 sherds coarse pottery
	Iron arrowhead
	5 flint blades and flakes
Ballywholan, County Tyrone	Leaf-shaped arrowhead
	Flint knife
	12 pieces of bone and a skull fragment
	4 sherds coarse pottery
Clonlum, County Armagh	Polished stone bead
	Potsherd
	V-shaped decorated comb
Ticloy, County Antrim	1 sherd undecorated pot
	Leaf-shaped arrowhead
	1 sherd decorated pot

Pottery from Ballykeel Portal Tomb, County Armagh

relative isolation from other prehistoric burial sites. Others are within clusters of megalithic tombs, usually of every tomb type.

A great example of a cluster is in north County Antrim, centred on Loughareema, also known as 'the vanishing lake'. Here, within a 2km radius of the lake, there are three portal tombs, four court tombs, three passage tombs and two wedge tombs – along with another 12 unclassified megalithic tombs. In addition to the megalithic tombs, there are a further 33 prehistoric burial sites, dating mainly to the Bronze Age. This activity suggests that Loughareema was part of a major sacred landscape throughout most of prehistory.

Other major clusters of megalithic tombs are located around Slieve Gullion in County Armagh and Ballygroll in County Londonderry.

It has been suggested that portal tombs were built close to routeways, and many are close to roads that are still in use. The tombs might have been intended as symbols of a strong and united local community.

Dating and finds

Given the small number of portal tombs that have been scientifically excavated, very few have been dated. However, the small number of radiocarbon dates available seem to show a period of construction and main use during the early Neolithic period. This is followed by occasional site disturbance, even up to the present day when some have been used as pig sties and even as stores for rubbish!

As with other megalithic tomb types, some portal tombs were re-used as burial sites during the Bronze Age. Ballykeel Portal Tomb in County Armagh is a good example.

Tirnony Portal Tomb, County Londonderry

A model of a portal tomb under construction

Here, a radiocarbon date of 1741–1525 BC was obtained from charcoal taken from a burial that had been placed into the cairn of the portal tomb.

Archaeologists believe that the chambers of most portal tombs were originally covered by a cairn, which left only the large capstones exposed. In most cases time has removed the above ground evidence for these cairns and they are only now revealed during excavation. In order to gain a more accurate picture of what portal tombs may have looked like, the modern visitor should try to picture a scene not unlike that shown here.

Where archaeologists have excavated portal tombs they have generally found Neolithic pottery, flint tools and stone beads. Only rarely do they find human remains, and these are usually traces of burnt bone and bone fragments.

These items are similar to those found in court tombs and seem to suggest that the two tomb types were being used at the same time and in the same way. It is not clear why people decided to build a portal tomb rather than a court tomb. Deciding to incorporate a huge capstone would make construction of portal tombs difficult, and they were not an 'easy' kind of tomb to build.

Analysis of the available dating information on portal tombs in Ireland, Wales and Cornwall suggests the first portal tombs and court tombs could have been constructed at around 4000–3800 BC, and almost certainly not later than 3600 BC.

Both tomb types had near continuous use for several hundred years after their construction and the dates from human bone from court tombs are not any earlier than the bone dates from portal tombs.

Ballykeel Portal Tomb, County Armagh

Portal tomb theories

Much of the early debate about the development of megalithic monuments centred on court tombs (see below) and passage tombs, as it was thought that portal tombs were a later degeneration of these. Recent studies have mostly focused on the positioning of portal tombs in the landscape in an attempt to understand the relationship between them and the other tomb types, the communities who built them and what part geography played in their location.

So despite their dramatic appearance and the length of time they have been on the Irish landscape, knowledge of these wonderful monuments is limited. Building an understanding of the portal tomb-building tradition must for now partly draw on the work that archaeologists have carried out at other types of megalithic monuments, particularly court and passage tombs. We do know that there are eight regions in Britain and Ireland where there are portal tombs. Most are in Ireland, with three separate and smaller groups in Cornwall and north and south Wales. Similar monuments are found elsewhere in north-west Europe, but regional variations exist here also.

There are certainly similarities between other types of megalithic tombs in Northern Ireland and elsewhere, but archaeologists believe the idea of erecting these large monuments of stone was most likely introduced from another part of Europe.

Ballyrenan Portal Tomb, County Tyrone

Ballylumford Portal Tomb, County Antrim

Court tombs

The court tombs of Northern Ireland have attracted a lot of attention from archaeologists. Ruaidhrí de Valera first produced a comprehensive review of court tombs throughout Ireland in 1960. In Northern Ireland, many were excavated between 1954 and 1976 by Dudley Waterman, Pat Collins and Estyn Evans. The results of their excavations still inform the debate about the monuments today.

A complete court tomb was scientifically excavated at Creggandevesky in County Tyrone between 1979 and 1982. Although the monument was barely visible before the excavation, it was found to be a very well-preserved tomb. As it had been hidden by blanket bog for so long it still contained its burials and artefacts. This monument was conserved and is now in state care.

In the past, court tombs have been given names such as chambered tombs, court cairns, lobster-claw cairns, horned cairns, court graves and gallery graves. Some have acquired local names, such as 'The Abbey' (Ballyboley, County Antrim) and 'County Carn' (Garvagh, County Tyrone) and many are referred to as giants' graves on maps and signposts.

Shape and form

In court tombs, there is normally a stone-built gallery consisting of between two and five chambers, usually separated from each other by stone slabs. The feature that gives this type of monument its name is the 'court', which consists of a row of upright

Annaghmare Court Tomb, County Armagh

Creggandevesky Court Tomb, County Tyrone

Annaghmare Court Tomb, County Armagh

stones at the entrance to the gallery. This forms a partially enclosed space, usually arranged in the shape of a semi-circle (but sometimes extending further).

At some sites, such as Annaghmare in County Armagh, dry-stone walling was found between the orthostats, presumably a method of preventing cairn material from falling between gaps in the stones into the court.

There is evidence from several court tombs, such as Creggandevesky, County Tyrone, that the gallery was roofed by overlapping slabs of stone (the technique used for this is known as 'corbelling') and that the roof was then covered by a flat-topped cairn of stones

that tapered away to the end of the cairn. The cairn stones were often kept in place by a row of 'kerb' stones.

There are many variations in the form and shape of court tombs. Some have two tombs constructed back to back, forming what is known as a dual court tomb; some were constructed front to front, forming what is known as a central court tomb.

The majority of court tombs throughout Northern Ireland have open courts. The average dimensions of simple open court tombs, including the cairn would be about 20m long by 10m. Some have distinctive features, such as gable-shaped stones at the end of the gallery, as at Ballywholan in

Annaghmare Court Tomb, County Armagh, reconstruction drawing: (A) forecourt, (B) chambers, (C) cairn, (D) corbelled roof, (E) corbel, (F) orthostats, (G) dry stone walling. (After Waterman, 1965.)

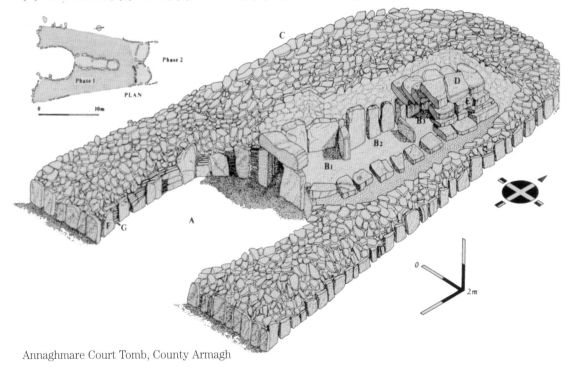

Annaghmare Court Tomb, County Armagh

43

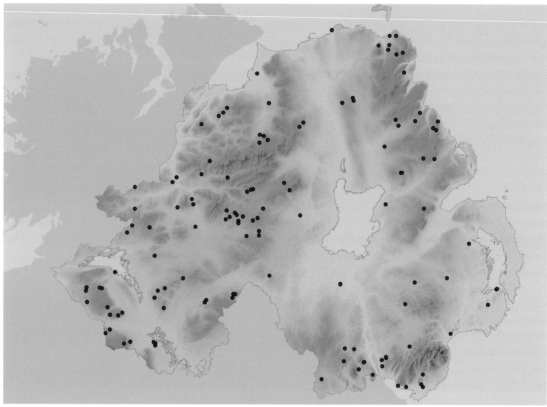

Distribution map of court tombs in Northern Ireland

County Tyrone, presumably to help support the corbelled roof over the chambers. Many court tombs have suffered severe damage since they were originally constructed and often lack a cairn, or even a court, as at Dunnaman in County Down. As a result, it is often difficult to determine the original shape and any later changes without careful excavation.

Location and positioning

In Northern Ireland, there are 126 known court tombs, mostly with single open courts, representing 30% of the 420 or so known across the whole of Ireland. There are 13 dual court tombs, with particularly fine examples at Audleystown in County Down and Aghanaglack in County Fermanagh. There is only one example of what is

Northern Ireland court tombs, by county

County	Court tombs	Possible court tombs
Antrim	26	0
Armagh	10	0
Down	16	2
Fermanagh	26	1
Londonderry	13	1
Tyrone	35	0
Total	**126**	**4**

Aghanaglack Dual Court Tomb, County Fermanagh

Dunnaman Court Tomb, County Down

45

Tully Court Tomb, County Fermanagh (under excavation)

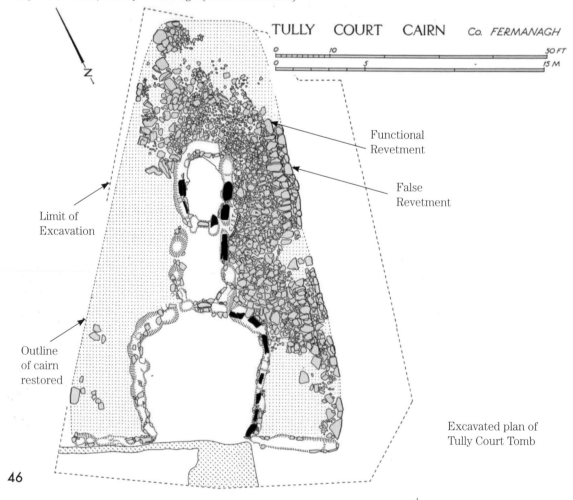

TULLY COURT CAIRN Co. FERMANAGH

Functional Revetment

False Revetment

Limit of Excavation

Outline of cairn restored

Excavated plan of Tully Court Tomb

possibly a central court tomb, located at Carrick East in County Londonderry.

Court tombs are found at a range of altitudes, from low-lying coastal areas to high on upland areas, but the greatest number (over 75%) lie between 100m and 250m above sea level. The distribution of court tombs by altitude is generally quite different to that of portal tombs. Apart from their occasional presence together in megalithic tomb clusters, court and portal tombs seem to be almost mutually exclusive in the landscape.

Court tombs tend to be built on platforms, knolls and small ridges with spectacular views over the surrounding countryside.

The broader court ends of single-court tombs are generally aligned in an easterly direction, mostly between north-north-east and south-east. They seem to have a close connection with the rising of the sun.

The reasons for the variations in locations are not fully understood. Just like the different built features of the tombs, their locations are probably more related to the needs and wishes of the local communities, and availability of suitable sites, than the need to comply with a special set of rules.

Carrick East Central Court Tomb, County Londonderry

Dating and finds

As with all types of megalithic monuments, it is not currently possible to securely date the actual stonework of court tombs. Archaeologists rely on radiocarbon dates obtained from their contents to provide some indication as to when the tombs were in use.

Radiocarbon dates from ten Northern Ireland court tombs, taken with other results

Examples of Northern Ireland court tomb finds

Site	Finds
Tully, County Fermanagh	Early Neolithic pottery chamber 1
	Stone bead chamber 2
	Partial flint javelin head chamber 2
	3 hollow scrapers in cairn and court
	Trimmed flint blade in court
	Bronze flat axe
	Cremated human bone (child 2-4 years) chamber 1
	Cremated human bone (young adult) chamber 2
	Cremated human bone (child 6-10) cist
Annaghmare, County Armagh	Undecorated carinated early Neolithic bowl sherds chamber 3
	Decorated Neolithic bowl sherds chambers 2 and 3
	Flint javelin head chamber 2
	15 scrapers, forecourt and gallery
	Smoky quartz fragment chamber 3
	Bear tooth
	Unburnt human bones of adult female and child
	Cremated human bones of adults and child
Ballymacaldrack, County Antrim	Leaf and lozenge shaped flint arrowheads
Dunloy, County Antrim	Decorated Neolithic carinated bowl sherds
	Plain Bronze Age vase urn
	Flint and quartz flakes
	Flint hollow and end scrapers, plano-convex knife, arrowhead fragment
	Pitchstone flake
	Cremated human bones: adult male 25-30 years, child 2 years and unknown number of others
Audleystown, County Down	Flint flakes, cores and scrapers. Plano-convex knives, javelin heads, leaf and lozenge arrowheads
	Worked quartz
	Fragments of plain Neolithic carinated and decorated bowls
	Burnt and unburnt human remains, representing 34 individuals. 4 children, 1 adolescent, 5 females 10 males and an assortment of unsexed adults
	Animal bones from 9 cows, 18 pigs, 11 sheep, 1 horse, 3 dogs and 1 bird

Ballymacaldrack Court Tomb, County Antrim

from elsewhere in Ireland, suggest that the tombs were being used between 5,900 and 5,600 years ago (3900–3600 BC).

More recent research has refined these dates to 3720–3560 BC. After this period, activity at court tombs ceased until the early Bronze Age, when many were re-used as burial sites. Radiocarbon dates also confirm that both court tombs and portal tombs were in use at the same time. They were contemporary tombs. Earlier and later radiocarbon dates also confirm that these sites attracted human activity over a much longer period, but this was not directly connected with the original court tomb builders.

At excavated sites, archaeologists usually find fragments of undecorated early Neolithic bowls. This is the same type of

pottery found at early Neolithic settlement sites, such as at Ballygalley in County Antrim.

Decorated pottery, usually found at later Neolithic sites, is also found at court tomb sites, suggesting that they were either constructed over a long period, or re-used by later generations. Other finds include flint artefacts, such as javelin heads, leaf-shaped arrowheads and hollow scrapers (a uniquely Irish flint tool). Occasionally, stone beads and porcellanite axe heads are also found.

Court tomb theories

Court tombs are found both in Ireland and Britain, with clusters in the north-east of Ireland, and the Clyde Valley and Galloway

Audleystown Dual Court Tomb, County Down

regions in Scotland. There are similar structures in north-west Europe, particularly in the Brittany area of France. This, along with evidence of trading, suggests that there was a network of contacts between Ireland and these areas during the Neolithic period. As a result there has been a lot of debate about the origins of court tombs and how their use may have spread to Ireland.

There are essentially two theories, both assuming that the tomb-builders originated in northern Europe. First, there is a cluster of court tombs, including some of the more elaborate types, around Sligo, Mayo and south Donegal. The concentration here has been taken to suggest that the tombs were introduced to that area first and developed before spreading east.

The second theory is that the tombs, in simple form, were introduced to the east of Ireland and became more elaborate as they were built, slowly moving in a westerly direction. It is perhaps more tempting to think that the original tomb-builders would have found it easier to sail up the Irish Sea and spread this concept of tomb building to western Britain and eastern Ireland, rather than to face the Atlantic swells to reach the west of Ireland first. But the lack of these tombs in the south-east of Ireland is puzzling – it would have been one of the first areas that could have been settled. Until more conclusive dating evidence is obtained, this debate will remain unresolved.

These monuments are known as tombs, and today we associate this with the burial of the dead. But it is clear that not everyone was being buried at these locations. Modern cemeteries have thousands of burials, representing all social levels of society, but court tombs generally hold the remains of only a few people.

Clearly, people at the time were being selective about who would be buried inside, and this has led to debate about religious practices and social hierarchies. The construction of the court itself suggests that the entrance area was a special space, marked out by the orthostats. It might have been an area used for some form of ceremonial activity.

Given the limited use of the sites for burials, one line of argument suggests that court tombs were not actually tombs at all, but rather ceremonial centres. They have been interpreted as places where the religious practices involved putting special bones and artefacts in the galleries. However, it is believed that Annaghmare Court Tomb in County Armagh was used only once, after which the court was blocked and no further use could have been made of it.

There are also interesting variations in the number of chambers within the gallery, from a minimum of two to a maximum of five. Sometimes chambers seem to have been left deliberately unused. Audleystown is a good example of this, as two of its chambers were found to be entirely free of bones and artefacts.

The artefacts found at these tombs are usually thought to be the items chosen by those carrying out the burial, and the artefacts were to accompany the dead into the afterlife. Some of the flint tools that have been found display signs of burning. Perhaps the body was cremated along with the person's favourite weapon. Or, in the case of javelin and arrowheads, were they the weapons that had caused death, and had been cremated inside the body of the deceased?

The dates achieved from radiocarbon and artefact analysis seem to point to portal and court tombs being among the earliest types of megalithic tombs that Neolithic people built, but a few Irish passage tombs have also produced early Neolithic dates.

Dromore Big Court Tomb, County Fermanagh

Passage tombs

West Torr Passage Tomb, County Antrim

Passage tombs can often be the most spectacular of the Neolithic megalithic tombs – certainly those at the Boyne Valley in County Meath are impressive, and are recognised internationally through their UNESCO World Heritage Site designation.

Passage tombs get their name from the passageway, formed by large upright stones, that connects the entrance of the tomb to an internal chamber. In some, the passage may be around 10m long, such as at West Torr in County Antrim, but in others, such as at Sess Kilgreen in County Tyrone, the passage may hardly be noticeable. Tombs like that at Sess Kilgreen are sometimes known as 'simple' passage tombs.

Passage tombs are generally covered by a circular mound of earth and stone called a cairn, which is often held in place by a ring of large boulders, or kerb stones.

Some passage tombs in Northern Ireland are sited on the top of hills commanding spectacular views over the surrounding countryside. They are often worth visiting for the views alone. While they are more modest than those at Newgrange or Knowth, Northern Ireland's passage tombs share most of the features that one might find in the Boyne Valley.

Slieve Gullion Passage Tomb, County Armagh

Inside Slieve Gullion Passage Tomb, County Armagh

Shape and form

The main feature of passage tombs is the stone chamber, which may stand alone or be divided into several different smaller chambers set off from a central area. There may be a passage lined with upright stones connecting the inner chamber to the outside of the monument. The passage and chamber is often still covered by a circular mound or stone cairn.

Usually, the cairn is contained within a ring of large stones, known as kerb stones. Some passage tombs contain examples of Neolithic artwork, in the form of spirals, circles and other patterns cut into the stonework.

The presence of so much visible stone, particularly in the body of the cairn, has led to the destruction of many passage tombs – the boulders provided a convenient source

Slieve Gullion Passage Tomb, County Armagh

Aerial view of Slieve Gullion Passage Tomb, County Armagh

of raw material for field walls and stones for country bridges and roads.

As with other megalithic tomb types, there are many variations in the form of passage tombs. The passage varies a lot, from the simple passage tombs noted above to the more elaborate examples. At Slieve Gullion in County Armagh, the passage is formed using dry-stone walling, found at many court tombs. The passage of other tombs is formed like a corridor of large, upright stones.

At some passage tombs the entrance faces towards either the winter or summer solstice.

Location and position

It has been estimated that there are about 230 passage tombs in Ireland, and most of these are located in a band extending from Sligo in the west, to the Boyne Valley in the east. There are 33 known passage tombs in Northern Ireland, representing around 15% of the total number in Ireland.

Passage tombs are often associated with mountain tops. There are well-known examples on Slieve Donard in County Down and Slieve Gullion in County Armagh. However, passage tombs are present at most altitudes in Northern Ireland, with a particular concentration (60%) between sea level and 200m above sea level. But their

Northern Ireland passage tombs, by county

County	Passage tombs	Possible passage tombs
Antrim	13	0
Armagh	6	2
Down	4	1
Fermanagh	2	1
Londonderry	1	0
Tyrone	8	0
Total	33	4

distribution on the landscape with regard to altitude is quite different from either portal tombs or court tombs.

You can also find these monuments located in what are referred to as passage tomb cemeteries. The Carrowmore cemetery in

County Sligo is very well known, and today it has at least 45 passage tombs. A Swedish archaeologist, Göran Burenhult, believes there once could have been as many as 200 tombs present there.

Large passage tomb cemeteries are few in number. So far, none have been found in Northern Ireland, but there is a small passage tomb cemetery in the townland of Sess Kilgreen in County Tyrone. Most of the monuments at the Sess Kilgreen complex have been badly damaged, and their former glory is not always easy to see. The complex is made up of the remains of at least four passage tombs, with another four located within ten miles of Sess Kilgreen.

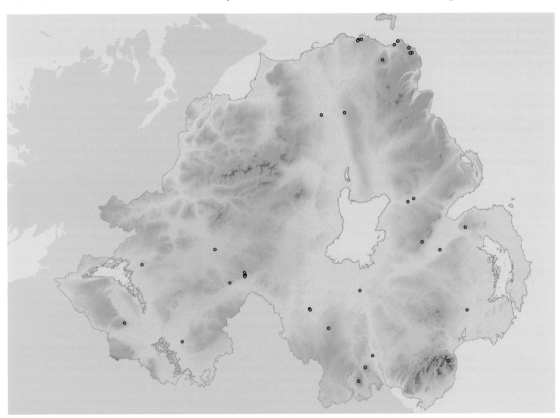

Distribution map of passage tombs in Northern Ireland

Sess Kilgreen – Neolithic art highlighted with chalk, County Tyrone

Currently, most passage tombs in Northern Ireland are located either in isolation or in clusters of other megalithic tombs and prehistoric burial monuments. A good example is the area around the north-east coast of Antrim, where there is a concentration of many types of megalithic tombs, including passage tombs.

Dating and finds

Radiocarbon dating evidence from the passage tomb cemetery at Carrowmore places the construction of some passage tombs at the very beginning of the Neolithic period at around 6,000 years ago (4000 BC), with additions at the site taking place for over a thousand years.

Excavations at passage tombs in Northern Ireland mostly took place before radiocarbon dating methods became available. Only Slieve Gullion in County Armagh has been dated by this method.

The passage tomb at Slieve Gullion was the only one in Northern Ireland shown to contain 'basin stones'. These are usually large oval-shaped stones, with a hollow chiselled into the upper surface, and some are highly decorated. There is a theory that basin stones were a ceremonial representation of 'saddle querns', which Stone Age people used every day to grind corn.

The usual type of pottery found at excavations in passage tombs is 'Carrowkeel

Neolithic leaf shaped flint arrowhead from Old Freehold, County Antrim

Bone or antler pins, stone balls, pendants and flint tools are also usually found in passage tombs, and occasionally, flint or stone mace heads.

Passage tomb theories

The origin of passage tombs in Ireland remains the subject of much debate and the contrasting theories share many similarities with those about court tombs.

Ware', named after another passage tomb cemetery in County Sligo where the pottery was originally identified. It is distinctive for its rich decoration in the form of grooves cut into the clay pots before they were fired.

There are examples of passage tombs in northern Europe. One on the island of Gavrinis, just off the coast of southern Brittany, has many similarities with tombs in Ireland. Following work at Carrowmore in County Sligo, one theory was proposed suggesting that indigenous people

Neolithic art at Knockmany Passage Tomb, County Tyrone

Examples of Northern Ireland passage tomb finds

Site	Finds
Magheraboy, County Antrim	Undecorated Neolithic pottery sherds
	Flint blades and flakes
	Burnt human bone
	Bronze Age pottery sherd from secondary deposit
Slieve Gullion, County Armagh	3 Basin stones
	Flint scrapers and chert flakes
	Barbed and tanged flint arrowhead
Sess Kilgreen, County Tyrone	Rock art
Knockmany, County Tyrone	Rock art
	Some cremated bone
	Flints
	Pottery sherd
Kiltierney, County Fermanagh	Rock art
	Leaf-shaped flint arrowhead
	Flint scrapers
	Decorated Neolithic pottery sherd

constructed the passage tomb cemeteries there in a comparatively simple style. As their descendants moved in an easterly direction, the tombs they built became more sophisticated, ending with the great passage tombs of the Boyne Valley in the east, representing the high point of passage tomb construction in Ireland.

However, another theory has been proposed that contradicts this one. It suggests that the major megalithic sites in the west of Ireland represented not the start but the end of the passage tomb tradition. The passage tomb builders entered Ireland at the Boyne Valley and constructed elaborate passage tombs such as Newgrange, Knowth and Dowth. Their descendants spread across Ireland in a westerly direction, with the quality of their tombs gradually degenerating along the way.

Passage tombs are perhaps the last of the megalithic tomb-types that are unambiguously Neolithic. Around 4,500 years ago (2,500 BC) just as some of the last passage tombs were being built, metalworking was being introduced into Ireland. This has been associated with the appearance of Beaker pottery, a distinctive style of highly decorated drinking vessel. Many bronze items and fragments of Beaker pottery have been found at the remaining type of megalithic monument, wedge tombs.

Passage tombs in six stages

In 1986, Alison Sheridan proposed a six-stage developmental process for passage tombs in Ireland. Stage 1 (3800-3400 BC) involved the construction of relatively small passage tombs, with kerb diameters of 10–15m. Most passage tombs in County Antrim would fall into this category.

Stage 2 (3600-3050 BC) saw the spread of passage tomb building to other areas of Ireland, while Stage 3 (3500-3050 BC) witnessed 'an escalation in the scale and complexity of tomb building'.

Stage 4 tombs had increased diameters, ranging from 26–50 metres, such as the one at the summit of Slieve Gullion in County Armagh. Stage 5, between 3100 and 2900 BC, saw the creation of the largest passage tombs, such as those in the Boyne Valley, with kerb diameters between 50 and 90 metres.

By Stage 6, a thousand years later than Stage 1, the passage tomb is surrounded by a range of monuments. An example can be found at Kiltierney in County Fermanagh, although some of the surrounding monuments were destroyed relatively recently during so-called land improvement schemes. Kiltierney is regarded as a centre of intense prehistoric activity.

Wedge tombs

Wedge tombs are the most numerous of all megalithic tomb types in Ireland. They are concentrated in the south-west, west and north-west of the island, with relatively few in the midlands or along the eastern seaboard.

In Northern Ireland there are 60 known wedge tombs. Most of them are in County Tyrone but there is a good example, known locally as Cloghnagalla, at Boviel in County Londonderry.

Wedge tombs display many of the features associated with other megalithic tombs, such as construction with massive stones and internal chambers that usually contain human remains. But they are often found to contain artefacts associated with Bronze Age societies. It seems either the megalithic building tradition continued into the early Bronze Age, or existing Neolithic tombs were later re-used.

Wedge tombs get their name from the overall shape of the monument; wide at the front, and tapering towards the rear; they look like a big wedge.

Shape and form

There is usually a single gallery, roofed with flat stone slabs and covered with a cairn of stones that is itself contained within an outer wall of boulders. Wedge tombs vary considerably in size and some have one or two additional chambers, sometimes referred to as end chambers, at the rear of the main gallery.

Bronze Age pots from Altanagh, County Tyrone

Top left: Cloghnagalla, or Boviel, Wedge Tomb, County Londonderry
Bottom left: Mountdrum Wedge Tomb, County Fermanagh

Loughash Wedge Tomb, County Tyrone

As with other megalithic tomb types, there is considerable regional variation. The presence of an outer wall which retained the cairn is found most often at wedge tombs in the north of Ireland. In County Clare wedge tombs have a more box-like appearance, being roofed over with one or two slabs of limestone. This is easier to achieve in that area, since the limestone slabs are found locally. These examples show how the construction techniques could be influenced by local geology.

A feature of many wedge tombs in Northern Ireland is the presence of a U-shape at the rear of the tomb. There are good examples at Kilhoyle and Boviel in County Londonderry and Loughash in County Tyrone.

Another feature seen at several wedge tomb excavations was the presence of a small end chamber. For example, at Loughash in County Tyrone, there are two end chambers at the rear of the tomb. They are separated from the main gallery by a 'septal' stone – a kind of dividing stone between the chambers. It is thought end chambers may have been a common feature of wedge tomb

construction, but are not usually seen due to the poor survival rates of these tombs.

Wedge tombs vary in length from a maximum of about 9m at Labbacallee in County Cork, to just 2m for those of the Burren area in County Clare. There are similar variations in Northern Ireland, where the tombs at Loughash and Boviel are 7m long, while a tomb at Ballybriest is only 3.3m.

Occasionally, a short portico or antechamber is located at the entrance, and a stone standing in the centre of the tomb is another feature of several wedge tomb sites in Northern Ireland, including Loughash.

As with most other megalithic tombs covered by a cairn of stones, people have helped themselves to a ready source of building material for stone work, field walls and road maintenance. From examples that have survived, it seems likely that wedge tombs were at one point surrounded by an oval, D-shaped or circular cairn of a height equivalent to the stone structure underneath.

Kilhoyle Wedge Tomb, County Londonderry

Location and positioning

There are 532 known examples of wedge tombs in Ireland as a whole. The 60 known wedge tombs in Northern Ireland represent just over 11% of the total on the island. Wedge tombs are not distributed evenly in Northern Ireland; most are in County Tyrone and there are none recorded at all in counties Armagh and Down.

However, when considering the distribution of wedge tombs, remember that most have not been archaeologically investigated, and just as with the other types of monuments it is possible that some of the classifications given are not correct. For example, at Moneycarragh, near Dundrum in County Down, there is a trapezoidal-shaped cairn, along with a few orthostats. This might be the remains of a wedge tomb, and as such is shown on the map below, but it would need to be excavated to find out for sure.

Northern Ireland wedge tombs, by county

County	Wedge tombs	Possible wedge tombs
Antrim	12	1
Armagh	0	0
Down	0	1
Fermanagh	11	0
Londonderry	13	2
Tyrone	24	3
Total	**60**	**7**

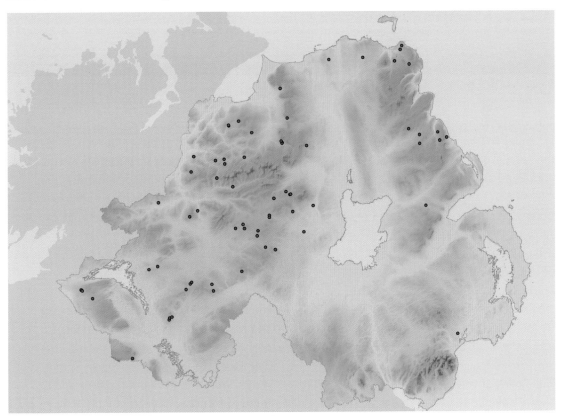

Distribution map of wedge tombs in Northern Ireland

Ballybriest Wedge Tomb, County Londonderry

The distribution of wedge tombs by altitude is similar to that for court tombs, with the majority (74%) located at between 105m and 250m above sea level. One notable exception is a reduction in numbers between 100m and 150m above sea level. As with the other megalithic tomb types, it has been suggested that the location of wedge tombs may be related to tribal territories in Ireland during the late Neolithic and early Bronze Age. They might be an indicator of the number of tribal groups at that time.

The fact that relatively few individuals seem to have been interred in these monuments might again suggest that not all members of the tribe could expect to be buried there. So those who were must have been specially chosen representatives of the tribe, or perhaps of a higher social status than the other members. Wedge tombs seem to indicate a time of significant change in social organisation.

Archaeologists have explored the relationship between the location of wedge tombs and soil fertility, as their sites in the west and south of Ireland seems to correspond with areas of lower quality soils. The study confirmed that many wedge tombs were found in poorer soils and at higher altitudes, but was unable to say why this should be.

Dating and finds

Relatively few wedge tombs have been excavated. Finds from them do little to clarify our knowledge of when they were first constructed and by whom. Many of the items found seem to date from the early Bronze Age, leading to much debate as to whether they were first constructed in the Neolithic and later re-used by Bronze Age people, or if they were a new kind of monument in the Bronze Age.

Finds from sites such as Boviel in County Londonderry, which include Neolithic and Bronze Age pottery, suggest that wedge tombs were constructed between the end of the Neolithic and into the early Bronze Age. The mould for an axe that was recovered from Loughash in County Tyrone would normally be associated with activity in the

Examples of Northern Ireland wedge tomb finds

Site	Finds
Loughash, County Tyrone	Mould for casting early Bronze Age axe
	Bronze blade
	Early Bronze Age pottery
	Cremated human bone
Ballybriest, County Londonderry	Beaker pottery
	Flint blade and fragments
	Granite hammerstone
	Cremated human bone
Clogherny, County Tyrone	Barbed flint arrowhead
	Cremated human bone
Largantea, County Londonderry	Neolithic pottery
	Beaker pottery
	Flint scrapers
	Cremated human bone
	Bronze blade
	Bone dagger plate
Boviel, County Londonderry	Cremated human bone
	Flint artefacts
	Neolithic pottery
	Bronze Age pottery

Clogherny Wedge Tomb, County Tyrone

65

middle Bronze Age, but may represent a later re-use of the site rather than reflect the period of initial activity.

The most numerous finds from wedge tomb excavations are sherds of pottery and a variety of types have been found. Beaker pottery, an important style that is closely associated with the early Bronze Age, has been recovered from several wedge tombs in Northern Ireland including Kilhoyle in County Londonderry, but this type of pottery is not usually found in wedge tombs in the south of Ireland.

Coarse, flat-bottomed undecorated pots were also found at Kilhoyle, as well as at Loughash (County Tyrone) and Largantea

Pottery sherds from Ballybriest Wedge Tomb, County Londonderry

(County Londonderry). Various examples of urns were also found at Kilhoyle, Largantea, Loughash and at Craigarogan in County Antrim. Although these are all pottery types from the Bronze Age, their existence at wedge tombs may signify the longevity of

Ballybriest Wedge Tomb, County Londonderry

66

Tireighter Wedge Tomb, County Londonderry

these monuments rather than the period of their original use. The dating difficulties are often made worse by disturbance at many wedge tombs.

Cremated and unburnt human bones have also been found in wedge tombs. While it would appear that cremation was the predominant burial rite, it may be that unburnt bone has simply not survived. The acidic soils mean that only some of the bones have survived for archaeologists to discover today.

Radiocarbon dates have only been obtained from one Northern Ireland wedge tomb and initially these seemed to suggest a construction phase at the transition between the later Neolithic and early Bronze Age.

Wedge tomb theories

Wedge tombs are often compared to the Allées Couvertes megalithic tombs in France, perhaps supporting the suggestion by

Large Bronze Age pot from Ballybriest Wedge Tomb, County Londonderry

Largantea Wedge Tomb, County Londonderry

archaeologist Ruaidhrí de Valera that Ireland was colonised from there during the Neolithic period, perhaps via landings in Cork and Kerry and spreading north and west.

However, the lack of direct evidence for this migration leaves open the possibility that wedge tombs were constructed by the indigenous people of Ireland, possibly influenced by ideas from the Continent or Britain.

Perhaps the most intriguing feature of wedge tombs is the presence of Beaker pottery at many sites. 'Beaker culture' is associated with the earliest appearance of metalwork in Ireland and a particular type

of pot. Usually the pots are highly decorated and found at sites all over Europe. This has fuelled speculation that the people who made them travelled as a way of life and traded in metal goods wherever they went. However, it has not yet been definitively established if it was people of the Beaker culture who built wedge tombs, or if they merely made use of what were already sacred monuments in the landscape.

Wedge tombs often contain human remains and it is this feature that has led to the classification of these monuments as tombs. They are not places of burial for the whole community, as the remains of only a few individuals are found in them.

At Ballybriest in County Londonderry analysis of the cremated human bone found in the tomb revealed that only around seven individuals had been placed inside. The bones displayed evidence of high-temperature burning, as in a funeral pyre. After cremation the bones were gathered up and placed inside the tomb, presumably as part of a burial ceremony.

However at Largantea Wedge Tomb in County Londonderry, the excavator found evidence suggesting that the cremation process was carried out inside the tomb and during its construction, but before the capstones had been put in place.

Despite the difficulties of placing the construction of wedge tombs in the late Neolithic or early Bronze Age, what is certain is that they marked the end of the megalithic tomb-building tradition.

Excavations at Ballybriest Wedge Tomb, County Londonderry

Tomb
Travelling

The best way to appreciate Northern Ireland's megalithic tombs is to get out and about to see them. Do a bit of 'tomb travelling'. Take a walk through thousands of years to the sites our ancestors chose as special – the ancients knew a good spot when they saw one. Visiting megalithic monuments is also a wonderful way to get acquainted with the countryside.

To start you on your way this section provides descriptions, directions and some details on 25 tombs, all of which are in State Care in Northern Ireland. Most are open all year round and are free of charge. The tombs are generally named after the townland in which they are located and every county of Northern Ireland is represented. Although some are in out-of-the-way places, most are relatively easy to get to and you can enjoy them at your leisure. Others are more difficult to find, but are well worth the effort, for the scenic location alone. Information boards placed near many of the tombs give extra details about the sites.

The NIEA, an agency within the Department of Environment, takes care of these sites, which are among 190 individual and groups of historic monuments in State Care in Northern Ireland. As well as the 25 highlighted here, there are hundreds of other megalithic sites dotted across the countryside. There is a full list of them at the end of the book. Some are 'scheduled' (protected against disturbance) monuments and most are on private farm land, where they are often protected by kind owners. So if you want to see any megalithic tombs

situated on private land, you must respect the landowners: ask for permission before entering their land, and take care for any livestock or crops.

To encourage you to get out and about and see as many sites as possible we provide some information about what's there and what other nearby monuments and attractions there are, in addition to the 'official' and local name of each tomb.

There are also SMR (Sites and Monuments Record) and grid reference numbers provided. The SMR will help you to access further information about the tombs on the NIEA website (see page 103 for instructions). To supplement the directions to the various megalithic sites, you can also enter the grid reference number into the Built Heritage Mapviewer service, available on the NIEA website (www.ni-environment.gov.uk), and generate and print out your own map.

When visiting the sites remember to wear strong footwear, and keep a watch on the weather. Please bear in mind that unless you have an excavation licence it is illegal to search for archaeological material, with or without a metal detector, by digging. Unauthorised metal detectors are prohibited from any protected monument. If you think that a monument has been damaged recently, the NIEA would be keen to find out about it, and can be contacted on the numbers and addresses shown on page 102.

Enjoy your tomb travelling!

Tirnony Portal Tomb, County Londonderry
Previous spread: Ballynoe Stone Circle, County Down

County Antrim

1. Ballylumford Portal Tomb

Also known as

'Druid's Altar', 'Ballylumford Dolmen'

Description

This attractive monument is unusually situated in the garden of an Edwardian farmhouse on the summit of a steep ridge on the peninsula of Islandmagee. Three basalt uprights support a substantial capstone that tilts along the top. Inside the chamber lies one further stone. Archaeologists have classified it as a portal tomb estimated to be around 5,500–5,800 years old, but think it may also be the chamber of a passage tomb. Excavation might clarify this in the future.

At the site

Wall plaque, parking

Nearby monuments and attractions

Islandmagee scenic drive, Brown's Bay, Whitehead Railway Museum, Carrickfergus Castle

Nearest towns and villages

Whitehead, Mill Bay, Islandmagee

Directions

From just past Whitehead on the A2 northwards, take the B90 north towards Ballylumford and follow this road for approximately 3 miles (5km) until you reach a crossroads. Staying on the B90, turn left at the crossroads and continue for a further 3 miles. You will see Ballylumford Portal Tomb on the right of the road just in front of a private house.

NIEA SMR number

ANT 041:007

Grid reference

D 4305 0160

2. Ballymacaldrack Court Tomb

Also known as
'Dooey's Cairn'

Description
This is a well preserved court tomb sited in peaceful countryside. Large upright stones border the deep U-shaped court, which leads to a stone chamber or 'cremation passage' where the burnt remains of five or six humans (male and female) have been found. Broken fragments of plain and decorated round-bottomed pottery bowls have also been excavated at the site, suggesting that some ritual may have taken place. Radiocarbon dating of the cremated remains put the tomb's age to around 3,800 BC.

At the site
Information board, easy access through a gate from the road

Nearby monuments and attractions
Craigs Passage Tomb, Craigs Court Tomb, Ballymoney Museum, Joey Dunlop Memorial Garden

Nearest towns and villages
Dunloy, Cloughmills, Ballymoney

Directions
From Dunloy, take the B16 south-east towards Cullybackey. About half a mile (1km) along this road, turn right into a minor road. Ballymacaldrack Court Tomb is a short distance along this road on the left.

NIEA SMR number
ANT 022:012

Grid reference
D 0215 1830

3. Craigs Passage Tomb

Also known as

'Craigs Dolmen'

Description

This tomb overlooks the Bann Valley and provides excellent views. It has eight closely set upright stones forming a single oval chamber, and a 3.5 tonne capstone. Lightning shattered the capstone in 1976 and it was repaired in 1985. An excavation at the time showed that the chamber was the remains of a passage tomb, not a portal tomb, as previously thought. Originally a cairn kept in place by a kerb would have covered the burial chamber, but it was removed in the mid-nineteenth century, when the chamber was explored and an urn holding cremation ashes was found.

At the site

Roadside parking

Nearby monuments and attractions

Ballymacaldrack Court Tomb, Craigs Court Tomb, Ballymoney Museum, Joey Dunlop Memorial Garden

Nearest towns and villages

Ballymoney, Dunloy, Rasharkin

Directions

From Ballymoney, take the B62 south towards Rasharkin. After approximately 4 miles (6.5km) turn left at Finvoy on to a minor road towards Dunloy. Follow this road for about 1 mile (1.5km) until you reach a small crossroads. Turn right here along the side of the hill and after about 1 mile (1.5km), you will see the passage tomb in a field on your right.

NIEA SMR number

ANT 022:024

Grid reference

C 9740 1728

County Armagh

4. Annaghmare Court Tomb

Also known as
'The Black Castle'

Description
This is one of the best built and preserved court tombs in Ulster. It is situated in a forestry plantation around Slieve Gullion close to the Armagh-Monaghan border. Large stones up to 1.9m high define the horseshoe-shaped court, which leads into a long triple-chambered burial gallery. An unusual feature in the court is a small standing stone to the south-east of the centre. Two portal stones mark the entrance to the gallery. Excavation finds at the site have included burned and unburned bone, flints, Neolithic pottery and teeth that probably belonged to a bear.

At the site
Information board, parking at gate on approach track

Nearby monuments and attractions
The Kilnasaggart Stone, Ballykeel Portal Tomb, Slieve Gullion Passage Tomb, walks and scenic drives in Slieve Gullion Forest Park, Slieve Gullion Courtyard, Bagenal's Castle, Newry and Mourne Museum

Nearest towns and villages
Newry, Cullyhanna, Crossmaglen

Directions
From Crossmaglen take the Carran Road, then B135 towards Cullyhanna for about half a mile (1km) and turn left at the crossroads into Annaghmare Road. This road bends around to the right and then the left. One quarter of a mile (0.5km) after this left-hand bend you will come to a track on the right signposted to the tomb. There is a small car park at the end of this track, close to the monument.

NIEA SMR number
ARM 027:007

Grid reference
H 9049 1782

5. Ballykeel Portal Tomb

Also known as
'Ballykeel Dolmen' 'The Hag's Chair'

Description
This is an attractive tripod portal tomb constructed during the Neolithic period and re-used for burial during the Bronze Age. It is located within the Ring of Gullion, an area rich in further megalithic sites and magnificent views. It has a huge capstone, supported on upright stones, over an octagonal burial chamber and the large trail of cairn material stretches back for around 25m. The chamber contained three finely worked and highly decorated 'Ballyalton' bowls. Excavations in 1963 found a Bronze Age cist burial in the cairn material close to the megalithic tomb.

At the site
Easy access and parking

Nearby monuments and attractions
Slieve Gullion Passage Tomb, walks and scenic drives in Slieve Gullion Forest Park, Slieve Gullion Courtyard, Bagenal's Castle, Newry and Mourne Museum

Nearest towns and villages
Newry, Mullaghbawn, Forkhill, Crossmaglen

Directions
From Newry follow the A25 west, through Camlough village and then take the B30 south towards Crossmaglen. Follow this for four miles (6.5km) until you reach Ballykeel where you will find signposts to the site. Turn left in Ballykeel (Mill Road) and then first left again into Ballykeel Road.

NIEA SMR number
ARM 028:020

Grid reference
H 9950 2132

6. Ballymacdermot Court Tomb

Description

Constructed around 3,500 BC, this is one of the best preserved court tombs in County Armagh and located in an area rich in prehistoric and historic monuments. Excavation in 1962 revealed three separate burial chambers, two of which contained cremated human bone. Evidence was also found that the tomb had been re-used for burial in the Bronze Age. A manoeuvring American tank slightly damaged the monument during World War II.

At the site

Wall plaque, parking

Nearby monuments and attractions

Clontygora Court Tomb, walks and drives in Slieve Gullion Forest Park, Killevy Church and Bagenal's Castle, Newry.

Nearest towns and villages

Newry, Camlough

Directions

From Newry, take the A1 south and then the B113 west. Take the first right turn and go straight across the next crossroads. When you arrive at a T-junction, turn right and you will see the monument 150m along this road.

NIEA SMR number

ARM 026:015

Grid reference

J 0656 2402

7. Clontygora Court Tomb

Also known as
'The King's Ring', 'The Long Cairn'

Description
This court tomb has a prominent position in the Slieve Gullion volcanic landscape and was constructed around 3,500 BC. It has an imposing façade of tall orthostats, some over 2.7m tall. Roof slabs and a large capstone over the first of three chambers are supported by enormous split granite boulders.

At the site
Wall plaque, parking

Nearby monuments and attractions
Walks and drives in Slieve Gullion Forest Park, Bagenal's Castle, Newry, Derrymore House, Bessbrook.

Nearest towns and villages
Newry, Jonesborough, Omeath

Directions
From Newry town centre, take the A1 south for about 4.5 miles (7km), then turn left into a minor road. Follow this road for about two miles (3km), where there is a sharp left turn. Follow this road for a short distance and you will see the monument signposted on the right.

NIEA SMR number
ARM 029:011

Grid reference
J 0987 1945

8. Slieve Gullion Passage Tomb

Also known as
'Calliagh Berra's House'

Description
This is one of the highest megalithic tombs in Ireland. It sits majestically near the top of Slieve Gullion at an altitude of 573m. There are extensive 360° views of the Ulster and Leinster countryside, taking in the Mourne Mountains, Carlingford Lough, the Cooley Peninsula and beyond. The extensive cairn covering the tomb was originally about 5m high. Unusually, the walls of this tomb are not made with large uprights but with stones a farmer might use to build a field wall. Finds in its passage and chamber have included cremated bone, flint and chert flakes, and a barbed and tanged arrowhead.

At the site
Information board

Nearby monuments and attractions
Ballykeel Portal Tomb, The Kilnasaggart Stone, walks and scenic drives in Slieve Gullion Forest Park, Slieve Gullion Courtyard, Bagenal's Castle, Newry and Mourne Museum

Nearest towns and villages
Newry, Mullaghbawn, Crossmaglen, Forkhill

Directions
From Newry, take the A1 south towards Dublin until you reach the roundabout at the Dublin Road Bridge. Follow the B113 and continue towards Meigh. Pass through

the village and after about 1km turn right to Slieve Gullion Forest Park. Once inside the forest park, follow the forest road and park at the first car park. From here there is a steep but rewarding climb to the top of Slieve Gullion, where the passage tomb is immediately visible.

NIEA SMR number
ARM 028:007

Grid reference
J 0246 2032

County Down

9. Audleystown Dual Court Tomb

Also known as
'Audleystown Cairn'

Description
This is a classic example of a dual court tomb. Situated near the shores of Strangford Lough, the tomb is set within a wedge-shaped cairn about 27m long. At either end is a shallow forecourt, each leading to a four-chambered gallery. An excavation in 1952 found the burnt and unburnt bones of 34 people of both sexes and all age groups, 17 in one gallery and 17 in another, as well as a selection of flint tools, pottery and food remains.

At the site
Information board, small car park

Nearby monuments and attractions
Audley's Castle, Castle Ward, Delamont Country Park, Exploris – Northern Ireland Aquarium (Portaferry)

Nearest towns and villages
Strangford, Downpatrick

Directions
From Downpatrick, follow the A25 towards Strangford. After about five miles (8km), turn left towards Audley's Castle. After about a mile and a quarter (2km), turn left down a minor road. There is a small car park a short distance down this road on the left. Park here and follow the path to the left. You will have to cross a couple of fields to reach the site.

NIEA SMR number
DOW 031:007

Grid reference
J 5619 5035

10. Ballynahatty Passage Tomb

Also known as

'The Giant's Ring', 'Ballynahatty'

Description

This interesting tomb is located near Belfast within the famous Giant's Ring, an impressive and atmospheric prehistoric earthwork circle. The Giant's Ring has a diameter of some 200 metres, with a 3.5m-high earthen bank enclosing the circle. Positioned slightly off centre in the ring, the passage tomb consists of five uprights roofed by a single capstone, enclosing a chamber. A slipped stone, now lying on edge, may have been a second capstone. Excavations at the tomb in 1917 proved that it had been disturbed by earlier digging, but abundant traces of cremated bone were found within it. The tomb appears to have been part of a ritual complex in the area.

At the site

Car park and easy access to monument

Nearby monuments and attractions

Giant's Ring Path, Lagan Meadows, Clement Wilson Park, Sir Thomas and Lady Dixon Park, Malone House and Barnett Demesne

Nearest towns and villages

Belfast, Lisburn, Edenderry

Directions

From Belfast, take the Upper Malone Road as far as Shaw's Bridge. Here, turn right into the B23 towards Lisburn and after about three quarters of a mile (1km) turn right into a minor road, signposted to the Giant's Ring. Follow this road and park in the car park at the end. Climb the path to the top of the bank and the passage tomb will be immediately apparent near to the centre.

NIEA SMR number

DOW 009:036

Grid reference

J 3272 6770

11. Goward Portal Tomb

Also known as
'Goward Dolmen', 'Cloghmore Cromlech', 'Pat Kearney's Big Stone, 'Finn's Fingerstones'

Description
This impressive portal tomb, located on the western foothills of the Mourne Mountains, was excavated shortly before 1834, when cremated bones and a flint arrowhead were found. The important natural history photographer R.J. Welch photographed the site in the nineteenth century, when a cottage was also visible, as was a man seated beside the monument – perhaps Pat Kearney himself. The remains of the cottage are visible as mossy-covered stones, just down-slope of the portal tomb.

At the site
Wall plaque, parking

Nearby monuments and attractions
Drumena Cashel and souterrain, Tollymore Forest Park, Mourne Mountains

Nearest towns and villages
Hilltown, Rathfriland

Directions
From Hilltown, take the B27 towards Newcastle and after about half a mile (1km) take the B8 north towards Kilcoo and Castlewellan. Follow this road for about 1.5 miles (2km) and take the second minor road on the right (Goward Road). Follow this road for about half a mile (1km) (signposted to Goward Dolmen).

NIEA SMR number
DOW 048:011

Grid reference
J 2437 3102

12. Kilfeaghan Portal Tomb

Also known as
'Kilfeaghan Dolmen'

Description
This impressive portal tomb has a capstone estimated to weigh 35 tonnes, supported by two portal stones, side wall and an end slab. It was constructed in the Neolithic from local granite and a long cairn of stones is also present. There is local knowledge of an unrecorded excavation in about 1912, when bones and pottery were said to have been found. Later investigations in the immediate area discovered flint scrapers and Neolithic pottery, presumably from the 1912 excavation.

At the site
Wall plaque, parking

Nearby monuments and attractions
Greencastle, Burren Heritage Centre, Kilkeel Portal Tomb, the Mourne Mountains

Nearest towns and villages
Rostrevor, Kilkeel

Directions
From Rostrevor, take the coast road (A2) towards Kilkeel for about 4.5 miles (7km). Just before Cassy Water Bridge, you will see a minor road to the left. Follow this road for about half a mile (1km), where you will see a signpost to the monument on your left. Park at the road and walk across two fields and you will see the portal tomb to your left.

NIEA SMR number
DOW 055:018

Grid reference
J 2322 1535

13. Legananny Portal Tomb

Also known as
'Legananny Dolmen', 'Giant's Grave'

Description
This striking tomb, splendidly sited on the upper slopes of Slieve Croob, affords magnificent views of the Mourne Mountains. Dating to about 5,500–5,800 years ago, it is an unusually tall tripod portal tomb – the two portal stones are 1.7m and 1.8m high and the capstone is 3m long. The single slab lying beneath the capstone may be a structural feature but may equally be among a deposit of boulders that form the base of a cairn. Slight traces of the cairn remain, but it was once far more extensive. Around the winter solstice the morning sun illuminates the entire underside of the capstone and tip of the backstone.

At the site
Information board, parking in lay-by beside lane leading to the monument

Nearby monuments and attractions
Drumadonnell Cross, Castlewellan Forest Park, St Patrick Centre (Downpatrick), Fergusons Irish Linen Centre (Banbridge)

Nearest towns and villages
Dromara, Castlewellan, Ballynahinch, Newcastle, Downpatrick

Directions
From Dromara, take the B7 towards Rathfriland for about 1 mile, turning left just past the village of Finnis. Follow this road for two miles, then straight ahead at a crossroads into Carrigagh Road. Then turn left at a T-junction into the Legananny Road for just over a mile. Turn left at another T-junction into Dolmen Road. Follow this until you reach a small lay-by and park there. Legananny portal tomb is a short distance up a laneway on the left.

NIEA SMR number
DOW 035:037

Grid reference
J 2887 4339

County Fermanagh

14. Aghanaglack Dual Court Tomb

Also known as
'Giant's Grave', 'Aghanaglack Dual Court Grave'

Description
This well-preserved dual court tomb is situated in a clearing in Ballintempo Forest, with lovely views across the Boho Valley. It is built across a south-facing slope and set within a rectangular cairn about 23m by 12m. There are two burial galleries, each of two chambers, flanked at each end by a roughly semicircular court. The tomb was found to contain Bronze Age and Stone Age items, pots, arrowheads and the remains of two children. Some of the artefacts are on display at the Enniskillen Museum.

At the site
Parking area and well maintained path to the site

Nearby monuments and attractions
Enniskillen Castle and Museums, Monea Castle, Cuilcagh Mountain Park, Marble Arch Caves Global Geopark, Devenish Island Monastic Site, Kingfisher Cycle Trail

Nearest towns and villages
Belcoo, Enniskillen

Directions
From Belcoo, take the B52 north-west towards Garrison. After approximately three quarters of a mile (1km), turn right towards Boho and travel along this road for 1 mile (1.5km), then turn left on to the Boho Scenic Route. Proceed for a further two miles (3km) and turn left into a minor road, which is signposted to the monument. Follow this minor road for approximately three quarters of a mile (1km) and follow the sign to the site.

NIEA SMR number
FER 210:034

Grid reference
H 0981 4358

15. Drumskinny Stone Circle, Burial Cairn and Stone Row

Description

This charming monument is not a megalithic tomb, but it is a very worthwhile site to visit as it demonstrates several of the many types of monuments associated with burial during the Bronze Age. Situated in an upland bog on the crest of a south-facing hill slope, the stone circle consists of 31 standing stones all under 2m tall, with some just a few centimetres in height. A row of small stones runs to a small low cairn in an alcove beside the circle. It is part of a complex of five sites in the immediate locality.

At the site

Car park close by

Nearby monuments and attractions

Lough Derg (Donegal), Ulster-American Folk Park, Omagh Historic Walking Trail, Castlederg Castle

Nearest towns and villages

Drumquin, Pettigo, Castlederg, Omagh

Directions

From Ederney, take the B72 north towards Castlederg and follow this road for approximately four miles (6.5km). At a staggered crossroads here, turn left on to a minor road and follow this road for approximately 1 mile (1.5km), where Drumskinny stone circle is signposted on the left.

NIEA SMR number

FER 135:003

Grid reference

H 2009 7072

County Londonderry

16. Ballybriest Wedge Tomb

Also known as
'Carnanbane'

Description
This tomb is located close to another megalithic tomb, dual court tomb (LDY 045:003). The wedge tomb is a small, but very good tomb example of this type of monument. It has two capstones and most of the inner walling still in place. The entrance is clearly visible, flanked by two portal stones.

At the site
Wall plaque, parking

Nearby monuments and attractions
Beaghmore stone circles, Davagh Forest

Nearest towns and villages
Draperstown, Cookstown

Directions
From Draperstown, take the B47 road west for about 1.5 miles (2.5 km). At the crossroads here, turn left on to the B162 and follow this for about 2.5 miles (4km) until you reach the Black Water Bridge. Here, turn left into a minor road and follow this for about half a mile (1km), where you will see Ballybriest Wedge Tomb and Ballybriest Dual Court Tomb on your right.

NIEA SMR number
LDY 045:002

Grid reference
H 7618 8845

17. Ballygroll Prehistoric Landscape

Description
This is a cluster of prehistoric monuments, several of which are in state care. They are presented as an interesting and accessible site, with paths and an information board explaining the monuments on display. The site includes megalithic tombs, burial cairns, barrows and cist burials, along with evidence of prehistoric field systems.

At the site
Information plaque, parking on road

Nearby monuments and attractions
Brackfield Bawn, Ness Wood Country Park

Nearest towns and villages
Claudy, Derry, Dungiven, Eglinton

Directions
From Claudy, follow the A6 road west until you see Burntollet Bridge and the entrance to Ness Wood Country Park. Take the next minor road on the right and follow this road for about two miles (3km) until you reach a crossroads. Go straight across and after a further mile (1.5km), you will see a small signpost to the site on the right of the road. Park here and follow the lane to the site, where an information board will detail the individual monuments present in the area.

NIEA SMR number
*LDY 023:037

Grid reference
*C 5330 1363

* As many individual monuments (such as stone circles and a stone row) are present at this site, the SMR and grid references represent the general area.

18. Knockoneill Court Tomb

Also known as

'Tamnybrack', 'Giant's Grave'

Description

This dramatic tomb is situated on high
ground on the eastern edges of the Sperrin
Mountains, with excellent views all around.
Dating from about 3,900–3,300 BC, it is
set within a rectangular cairn with a semicircular court of upright stones leading
to a gallery consisting of two chambers.
This court tomb is unusual in that it has
a subsidiary chamber at the back of the
gallery, which is entered via a passage in
the side of the tomb. It seems to have been
built in the Neolithic period and re-used in
the Bronze Age. Finds at the site include
Neolithic and Bronze Age pottery in the
main chambers and a cremation and pits
with pottery in the court.

At the site

Information board

Nearby monuments and attractions

Tammyrankin Court Tomb, Ballintemple
Bullaun Stone, Garvagh Museum and
Heritage Centre

Nearest towns and villages

Garvagh, Swatragh, Dungiven

Directions

From Swatragh, take the Drumbane Road
towards Brockaghboy to the north-west
(North Sperrin Scenic Route). Travel along
this road for just over two miles (3km)
and turn left into the Knockoneill Road.
Knockoneill Court Tomb is about half a mile
along this road on the right hand side at the
top of a small hill.

NIEA SMR number

LDY 026:052

Grid reference

C 8196 0875

19. Tamnyrankin Court Tomb

Also known as
'Tamnyrankin Cairn'

Description
This is a very good example of a court tomb with the bonus of commanding views over the surrounding countryside. The well-preserved monument has an impressive court and a gallery with two chambers leading off it, displaying many interesting features such as jamb and sill stones and the remains of the corbel stones that once covered the gallery. A further gallery is located at the rear of the stone cairn. Excavation in 1940 revealed Neolithic decorated bowls, flint tools and the cremated remains of an adult human.

At the site
Wall plaque, parking

Nearby monuments and attractions
Knockoneill Court Tomb, Tirnony Portal Tomb

Nearest towns and villages
Swatragh, Garvagh, Kilrea, Maghera

Directions
From Swatragh, take the A29 road north towards Garvagh. After about 1.5 miles (2.5km), you will see a minor road (Tamnyrankin Road) on your left. Follow this road for about three quarters of a mile (1.3km) and you will see a lane and small direction sign on your right. Follow this lane for about half a mile (1km), through what appears to be a farmyard and you will arrive at the site.

NIEA SMR number
LDY 026:013

Grid reference
C 8338 1029

20. Tirnony Portal Tomb

Also known as
'Tirnony Dolmen'

Description
This fine 5,000 to 6,000 year-old portal tomb is situated right on the side of a minor road. It consists of a single chamber covered by capstone, supported by three of the six upright stones, two of which form the portal. Weathering caused the capstone to fall to the ground in 2010 and archaeologists began excavating the site (the first portal tomb excavation in Northern Ireland in 45 years) in advance of repair and restoration work. Finds from the chamber include flint tools and sherds of undecorated early Neolithic pottery.

At the site
Roadside parking

Nearby monuments and attractions
Tirkane Sweat House, Tullyheran Fort, Maghera Church and Round Tower, Bellaghy Bawn

Nearest towns and villages
Maghera, Magherafelt, Swatragh

Directions
From the centre of Maghera, follow the Tirkane Road to the north-west for approximately one mile (1.5km), then turn right into Tirnony Road. The tomb is a short distance along this road on the right.

NIEA SMR number
LDY 036:010

Grid reference
C 8404 0173

County Tyrone

21. Ballywholan Portal Tomb

Also known as
'Carnfadrig', 'Carnpatrick' (Patrick's Cairn)

Description
This complex and enigmatic monument, situated on a wooded hill near the Tyrone-Monaghan border, is classified as a portal tomb with subsidiary chambers because it combines elements of both portal and court tombs. It consists of a 27m-long rectangular cairn with a large chamber at its east end and two chambers at the west end running north-south. The settings of stones within the cairn are puzzling. The site was excavated in 1899 and finds included cremated bones, ashes, flints and an arrowhead. But the main body of the cairn has not been excavated and there may be other hidden chambers.

At the site
Roadside lay-by parking

Nearby monuments and attractions
Ballywholan Dual Court Tomb, Clogher Hillfort

Nearest towns and villages
Clogher, Augher

Directions
From Clogher, take the B83 south towards Monaghan. After about three miles (5km), turn right into a minor road and follow this for approximately three quarters of a mile (1km). Ballywholan Portal Tomb is in a small forest to the right.

NIEA SMR number
TYR 065:003

Grid reference
H 5554 4899

22. Cregganconroe Court Tomb

Description
This tomb is located in a prominent position in an area of eskers, which are long gravel ridges deposited by retreating glaciers or ice sheets from the Ice Age. A gallery of two chambers, which has one large capstone remaining, leads off the remains of the court and two separate chambers are located at the rear, in what would have been the cairn.

At the site
Wall plaque, parking

Nearby monuments and attractions
Creggandevesky Court Tomb, An Creagán visitor centre, Ulster American Folk Park.

Nearest towns and villages
Pomeroy, Carrickmore, Omagh, Cookstown

Directions
From the An Creagán visitor centre on the main A505 Cookstown to Omagh Road, take the minor road towards Pomeroy and follow this for about 2 miles (3km) until you reach a crossroads. Turn left here and follow this road for just over a mile (1.5km), where you turn right (at Cam Lough). About half a mile along this road you will see a lane. Park here and walk to the site.

NIEA SMR number
TYR 037:01

Grid reference
H 6634 7588

23. Creggandevesky Court Tomb

This very well preserved court tomb dated to about 3500 BC sits on a hill with commanding views over Lough Mallon. It has an impressive lintel stone over its entrance portal between the court and the three burial chambers in the gallery. The tomb decreases in height from front to back and the chambers follow accordingly. The 18m-long, wedge-shaped (trapezoidal) cairn is also in good condition. Its retaining walls still stand to some height and a few of the roof stones are still in position. An excavation in 1982 revealed traces of the burnt bones of at least 21 people, flint tools and Neolithic pottery.

At the site
Roadside parking
Nearby monuments and attractions
Cregganconroe Court Tomb, Killucan Wedge Tomb, An Creagán Visitor Centre, Ulster-American Folk Park
Nearest towns and villages
Carrickmore, Cookstown, Omagh
Directions
From Cookstown, take the A505 towards Omagh and travel along this road for about 12 miles (19km). Take the minor road towards Pomeroy, on the left just before the An Creagán Centre. Continue along this road for about two and a half miles (4km), passing through two crossroads. There is a very small car park on the right hand side of the road, with Lough Mallon visible to the right. Keeping the lake to your right, follow the shore until you reach the court tomb on a small hill at the western end of the lake.
NIEA SMR number
TYR 037:014
Grid reference
H 6460 7500

24. Glenknock Portal Tomb

Also known as
'Druid's Altar', 'Cloghogle'

Description
This monument is defined by two portal stones and a backstone. The capstone was recently damaged during agricultural reclamation work close to the site.

At the site
Wall plaque, parking

Nearby monuments and attractions
Newtownstewart Castle, Harry Avery's Castle, Ulster American Folk Park

Nearest towns and villages
Newtownstewart, Douglas Bridge, Victoria Bridge, Ardstraw

Directions
From Newtownstewart, take the B165 road towards Douglas Bridge, but immediately after crossing the Strule River, turn right into the B47 towards Plumbridge. After about half a mile (1km), turn left into a minor road and follow this road for about a mile (1.5km). You will see the portal tomb on your right.

NIEA SMR number
TYR 017:009

Grid reference
H 4118 8794

25. Knockmany Passage Tomb

Also known as
'Annia's Cove'

Description
This tomb is located on the summit of a hill in Knockmany Forest Park, with superb views over the Clogher Valley. The principal stones are 1–2m high, forming a wedge shaped chamber. Several are engraved with circles, zigzags and spirals – exceptionally interesting passage grave art and perhaps the best examples of this art in Ulster. In 1959 the government heritage service added a covering cairn and glass structure to protect the stones from weathering and vandalism. In its present state the cairn is an almost circular mound about 25m in diameter.
You can see the stones through a gate and anyone wishing to examine them in detail can contact the NIEA on 028 3885 1102 to arrange for the chamber to be opened.

At the site
Car parks nearby

Nearby monuments and attractions
Clogher Hillfort, Errigal Keerogue Cross and Church, Knockmany Forest Park, The Carleton Trail

Nearest towns and villages
Augher, Clogher

Directions
From Augher, take the minor road north towards Seskinore and after about two miles (3km) you will reach a five-road junction where the minor road meets the B83. Enter Knockmany Forest at this point on the right and follow the forest road and signposts to Knockmany Passage Tomb, which is located at the top of the hill.

NIEA SMR number
TYR 059:001

Grid reference
H 5469 5590

The Giant's Ring, Ballynahatty

Further Reading and Resources

Books

Landscapes of Neolithic Ireland
Cooney, G, 2000. London: Routledge

Living Places, Archaeology, Continuity and Change at Historic Monuments in Northern Ireland
Donnelly, CJ, 1997. Belfast: Institute of Irish Studies

Pieces of the Past: Archaeological Excavations by the Department of the Environment
Hamlin, AE and Lynn, CJ, 1988. Belfast: HMSO

Temples of Stone, Exploring the Megalithic Tombs of Ireland
Jones, C, 2007. Cork: Collins

The Archaeology of Ulster from Colonisation to Plantation
Mallory, JP and McNeill, TE, 1991. Belfast: Institute of Irish Studies

Ireland's Ancient Stones, a Megalithic Heritage
McNally, K, 2006. Belfast: Appletree Press

Battles, Boats and Bones, Archaeological Discoveries in Northern Ireland 1987-2008
Murray, E and Logue, P, (Eds), 2010. Belfast: Northern Ireland Environment Agency and TSO

An Archaeological Survey of County Armagh
Neill, K, 2009. Belfast: TSO and NIEA

A Guide to the Historic Monuments of Northern Ireland in State Care
Northern Ireland Environment Agency, 2009. Belfast: TSO

Irish Megalithic Tombs
Shee Twohig, E, 1990. Princes Risborough: Shire Publications

Useful web sites

The Northern Ireland Environment Agency: Built Heritage
www.ni-environment.gov.uk

Centre for Archaeological Fieldwork, Queen's University, Belfast
www.qub.ac.uk/schools/CentreforArchaeologicalFieldworkCAF

Centre for Maritime Archaeology, University of Ulster
**http://www.science.ulster.ac.uk/esri/Centre-for-Maritime-Archaeology,65.
html#page=introduction**

Archaeology associations and societies

Ulster Archaeological Society
New members are always welcome
c/o School of Geography Archaeology and Palaeoecology
Queens University Belfast
42 Fitzwilliam Street
Belfast BT9 6AX
http://uas.society.qub.ac.uk.
Email: arcpal@qub.ac.uk

Federation for Ulster Local Studies
Can provide details of many local historical societies
18 Ardmore Avenue
Downpatrick
County Down
BT30 6JU
http://www.fuls.org.uk.
Email: info@fuls.org.uk

Museums
Northern Ireland Museums Council
6 Crescent Gardens,
Belfast,
BT7 1NS
www.nimc.co.uk
Tel: +44 028 9055 0215
The Northern Ireland Museums Council carries details, including the opening times of every museum in Northern Ireland. Many county museums have small collections of interesting prehistoric artefacts.

Ulster Museum
Botanic Gardens
Belfast BT9 5AB
www.nmni.com/um
Telephone 0845 608 0000

National Museum of Ireland
Kildare Street
Dublin 2
www.museum.ie
Telephone 00353 1 6777444

NIEA contacts

Contact	Telephone	Fax	Email
Built heritage general enquiries	028 9054 3159	028 9054 3111	bh@doeni.gov.uk
Historic buildings general enquiries	028 9054 3095	028 9054 3150	bh@doeni.gov.uk
Historic buildings listing enquiries	028 9054 3055 or 028 9054 3075	028 9054 3150	bh@doeni.gov.uk
Historic monuments general enquiries	028 9054 3159	028 9054 3111	hmenquiries@doeni

How to use the NIEA Sites and Monuments Records (SMR) database

The SMR database is available online at this address: http://apps.ehsni.gov.uk/ambit

The database holds information on over 16,000 archaeological sites and historic monuments, including all of the megalithic tombs listed in this book.

To find further information on any of the tombs listed, look up the number and key in the relevant SMR, as shown.

1 Type in this URL (web site address) into your browser

2 Enter the three-letter county code from the SMR number of the tomb you want to look up, for example ANT

3 Enter the first part of the SMR number

4 Enter the second part of the SMR number

5 Click 'Search'

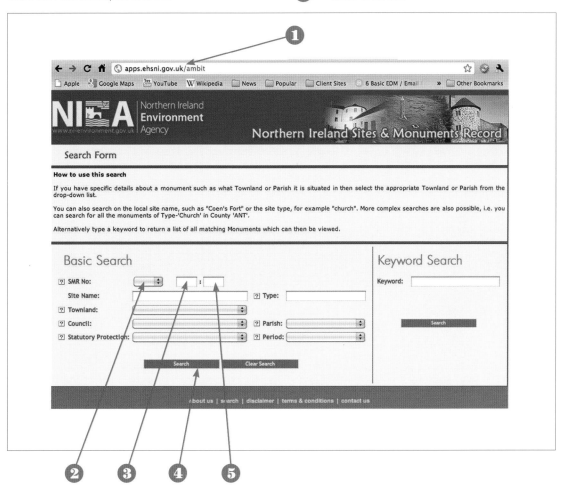

List of Megalithic Tombs in Northern Ireland

The following is not a list of individual megalithic tombs – it provides details of SMR sites, as classified by the NIEA. There may be more than one monument at an SMR site, or a variety of monuments. For example, at Davagh Lower in County Tyrone (SMR number TYR 020:009), there is a megalithic tomb, stone circles and stone rows. The highlighted entries in the list are the monuments described in the 'Tomb Travelling' section.

County Antrim		
Tomb type	Townland	SMR number
Court tombs	Antynanum	ANT 029:092
	Ardihannon	ANT 003:056
	Ballyalbanagh	ANT 039:023
	Ballyboley	ANT 040:018
	Ballymacaldrack	ANT 022:012
	Ballymarlagh	ANT 038:002
	Ballymena	ANT 028:019
	Ballyutoag	ANT 056:024
	Ballyvennaght	ANT 009:117
	Ballyvoy	ANT 005:003
	British	ANT 055:111
	Broom-Beg	ANT 009:033
	Browndod	ANT 044:035
	Browndod	ANT 044:037
	Craigban	ANT 009:038
	Craigs	ANT 022:023
	Doonan	ANT 029:005
	Drains Bog	Not in SMR
	Dunloy	ANT 022:010
	Dunteige	ANT 035:030
	Eglish	ANT 009:029
	Glenmakeeran	ANT 009:024
	Lisnahay South	ANT 030:017
	Loughconnelly	ANT 033:011
	Lubitavish	ANT 019:006
	Tervillin	ANT 005:016
Passage tombs	Aghaleck	ANT 008:001
	Ballintoy Demesne	ANT 004:013
	Ballycollin	ANT 064:001
	Ballyvoy	ANT 005:004
	Clegnagh	ANT 004:012
	Craigs	ANT 022:024
	Cross	ANT 005:006
	Cushleake Mountain North	Not in SMR

County Antrim		
Tomb type	Townland	SMR number
Passage tombs	East Torr	ANT 010:001
	Kilmakee	ANT 050:060
	Lemnagh Beg	ANT 004:011
	Templepatrick	ANT 051:058
	West Torr	ANT 009:019
Portal tombs	Ballygawn	ANT 035:036
	Ballylumford	ANT 041:007
	Ballyvennaght	ANT 009:020
	Ballyvennaght	ANT 009:021
	Ballyvennaght	ANT 009:022
	Ticloy	ANT 029:031
Wedge tombs	Ault , alias Gowkstown	ANT 029:019
	Ballyruther	ANT 030:014
	Ballyvennaght	ANT 009:023
	Beardiville	ANT 006:003
	Buckna	ANT 034:049
	Craigarogan	ANT 051:040
	Craigban	ANT 009:203
	Curramoney	ANT 008:018
	Dunmakelter	ANT 009:207
	Dunteige	ANT 035:002
	Longmore	ANT 028:007
	Tamybuck	ANT 029:039
Unclassified megalithic tombs	Aghafatten	ANT 028:025
	Aghaleck	ANT 009:184
	Aghaleck	ANT 009:191
	Aghalee	ANT 062:040
	Aghalee	ANT 062:041
	Aghalislone	ANT 064:047
	Altigarron	ANT 060:017
	Araboy	ANT 003:110
	Ballintoy Demesne	ANT 004:109
	Ballsallagh	ANT 024:036
	Ballyalbanagh	ANT 045:048

Knockmany Passage Tomb

County Antrim		
Tomb type	**Townland**	**SMR number**
Unclassified megalithic tombs	Ballyalbanagh	ANT 045:042
	Ballybracken	ANT 046:009
	Ballycleagh	ANT 015:017
	Ballycraig Lower	ANT 006:016
	Ballycraig Lower	ANT 006:017
	Ballycraig Lower	ANT 006:009
	Ballyellough	ANT 063:062
	Ballyellough	ANT 063:060
	Ballygowan	ANT 040:020
	Ballygowan	ANT 046:012
	Ballygowan	ANT 040:022
	Ballygowan	ANT 046:038
	Ballyhome	ANT 006:032
	Ballymacaldrack	ANT 022:049
	Ballyminstra	ANT 037:042
	Ballynastraid	ANT 003:090
	Ballynastraid	ANT 003:091
	Ballyoglagh	ANT 007:096
	Ballypitmave	ANT 059:081
	Ballyreagh	ANT 027:077
	Ballyreagh	ANT 027:084
	Ballyreagh Upper	ANT 005:032
	Ballyrickard Beg	ANT 040:024
	Ballyruther	ANT 035:055
	Ballyteerim	ANT 015:020
	Ballyveely	ANT 009:032
	Ballyveely	ANT 009:101
	Ballyveely	ANT 009:107
	Ballyveely	ANT 009:036
	Barnish	ANT 043:041
	Bay	ANT 029:082
	Bighouse	ANT 009:018
	Browndod	ANT 044:027
	Browndod	ANT 044:028
	Caherty	ANT 033:051
	Caherty	ANT 033:038
	Carnduff	ANT 040:009
	Carnlelis	ANT 008:157
	Carnloughern	ANT 067:009
	Cloghs	ANT 019:007
	Cloghs	ANT 019:008
	Corrymeelagh	ANT 010:003

County Antrim		
Tomb type	**Townland**	**SMR number**
Unclassified megalithic tombs	Corvally	ANT 009:187
	Craig	ANT 007:093
	Craigfad	ANT 009:203
	Croaghmore	ANT 007:131
	Cross	ANT 005:024
	Curragh Knocknacarry	ANT 015:011
	Dickeystown	ANT 029:099
	Donegore	ANT 050:031
	Doonbought	ANT 027:082
	Drumacullin	ANT 009:176
	Drumacullin	ANT 009:199
	Drumadarragh	ANT 045:065
	Drumadarragh	ANT 045:066
	Drumadoon	ANT 009:123
	Drumagorgan	ANT 050:027
	Drumavoley	ANT 009:100
	Drumeeny	ANT 009:182
	East Torr	ANT 010:007
	East Torr	ANT 010:029
	East Torr	ANT 010:030
	Evishnablay	ANT 024:006
	Galboly Lower	ANT 020:059
	Galboly Lower	ANT 020:061
	Galboly Lower	ANT 020:060
	Glenaan	ANT 019:005
	Glenmakeeran	ANT 009:056
	Glenmakeeran	ANT 009:202
	Glenmakeeran	ANT 009:055
	Glenmakeeran	ANT 009:147
	Grange of Carmavy	ANT 055:115
	Grange of Inispollan Mountain	ANT 015:034
	Greenan	ANT 009:167
	Islandahoe	ANT 012:040
	Kilgreel	ANT 051:044
	Kilrobert	ANT 009:189
	Knocksoghey	ANT 004:103
	Knocksoghey	ANT 004:107
	Layd	ANT 015:022
	Legoniel	ANT 060:016
	Legoniel	ANT 060:018

Top right: Druid's Stone, White Park Bay, County Antrim

Right: Ballymacdermot Court Tomb, County Armagh

County Antrim		
Tomb type	**Townland**	**SMR number**
Unclassified megalithic tombs	Lemnagh Beg	ANT 004:084
	Lemnagh More	ANT 003:103
	Lisbellanagroagh Beg	ANT 003:097
	Lisbellanagroagh Beg or More	ANT 003:098
	Lisbreen Half Quarter	ANT 028:065
	Livery Lower	ANT 012:050
	Lossett	ANT 009:028
	Moyadam	ANT 051:006
	Moyarget Upper	ANT 008:024
	Moyaver Upper	ANT 013:027
	Oldstone	ANT 050:086
	Revallagh	ANT 006:057
	Straid	ANT 046:037
	Tehorny	ANT 026:020
	Tervillin	ANT 005:012
	Tervillin	ANT 005:015
	Tirkilly	ANT 014:009
	Tobergill	ANT 044:041
	Tobergill	ANT 050:032
	Torglass	ANT 009:142
	Lower Tullykittagh	ANT 027:098
	Lower Tullykittagh	ANT 027:099
	Lower Tullykittagh	ANT 027:100
	Twenty Acres	ANT 009:139
	Upper Tullykittagh	ANT 023:028
	Upper Tullykittagh	ANT 023:038
	Upper Tullykittagh	ANT 023:053
	Upper Tullykittagh	ANT 023:056
	Upper Tullykittagh	ANT 023:057
	Upper Tullykittagh	ANT 023:058
	West Division	ANT 052:074
	West Division	ANT 052:076
	West Division	ANT 052:077
	White Park	ANT 004:091

County Armagh		
Tomb type	**Townland**	**SMR number**
Court tombs	Annacloghmullin	ARM 025:010
	Annaghmare	ARM 027:007
	Ballintaggart	ARM 009:006
	Ballintaggart	ARM 009:026
	Ballymacdermott	ARM 026:015
	Ballymacdermott	ARM 026:048
	Carrickananny	ARM 025:019
	Clonlum	ARM 029:004
	Clontygora	ARM 029:011
	Eshwary	ARM 026:022
Passage tombs	Ballybrolly	ARM 012:007
	Ballybrolly	ARM 012:008
	Carnavanaghan	ARM 016:028
	Carnbane	ARM 026:019
	Cross	ARM 026:012
	Slieve Gullion	ARM 028:007
Portal tombs	Aughadanove	ARM 028:004
	Aughnagurgan	ARM 024:002
	Ballykeel	ARM 028:020
	Clonlum	ARM 029:005
	Lagan	ARM 019:019
Unclassified megalithic tombs	Aghadavoyle	ARM 029:034
	Annaghmare	ARM 027:011
	Aughnagurgan	ARM 024:001
	Aughnagurgan	ARM 024:008
	Carganamuck	ARM 008:017
	Carnbane	ARM 026:046
	Carran	ARM 030:006
	Clontygora	ARM 029:012
	Clontygora	ARM 029:024
	Drumacanver	ARM 015:034
	Duvernagh	Not in SMR
	Latbirget	ARM 028:002
	Lisadian	ARM 012:049
	Meigh	ARM 029:035
	Outleckan	ARM 025:020
	Terraskane	ARM 012:046
	Tullynavall	ARM 028:026
	Tullyvallan	ARM 024:011
	Tullyvallan	ARM 024:012
	Tullyvallan	ARM 024:013

Top right: Goward Portal Tomb, County Down

Right: Legananny Portal Tomb, County Down

County Down		
Tomb type	**Townland**	**SMR number**
Court tombs	Audleystown	DOW 031:007
	Aughnagon	DOW 051:004
	Ballinran	DOW 054:012
	Ballintur	DOW 055:050
	Ballyalton	DOW 038:006
	Ballynichol	DOW 010:041
	Ballyrogan	DOW 055:022
	Burren	DOW 051:031
	Carnew	DOW 028:057
	Dunnaman	DOW 055:030
	Edenmore	DOW 047:090
	Glasdrumman	DOW 022:033
	Goward	DOW 048:030
	Lappoges	DOW 021:029
	Milltown	DOW 051:011
	Moyad	DOW 055:052
Passage tombs	Annadorn	DOW 030:007
	Ballaghbeg	DOW 049:011
	Ballynahatty	DOW 009:036
Portal tombs	Annacloy	DOW 030:033
	Ballynahatten	DOW 057:007
	Goward	DOW 048:011
	Greengraves	DOW 005:028
	Kilfeaghan	DOW 055:018
	Kilkeel	DOW 056:025
	Legananny	DOW 035:037
	Loughmoney	DOW 031:002
	Slievenagriddle	DOW 038:015
	Wateresk	DOW 043:061
Unclassified megalithic tombs	Ardtole	DOW 045:004
	Audleystown	DOW 031:049
	Aughnahoory	DOW 056:020
	Ballyedmond	DOW 054:014
	Ballygraffan	DOW 010:033
	Ballygraffan	DOW 010:035
	Ballylesson	DOW 009:051
	Ballynahatty	DOW 009:037
	Ballynahatty	DOW 009:050
	Ballyveagh Beg	DOW 056:007
	Brackenagh East	DOW 056:006
	Coolnacran	DOW 034:086
	Crobane	DOW 047:058

County Down		
Tomb type	**Townland**	**SMR number**
Unclassified megalithic tomb	Crobane	DOW 047:058
	Derrydrummuck	DOW 034:090
	Derryleckagh	DOW 051:009
	Drumadonnell	DOW 035:054
	Glasdrumman	DOW 053:002
	Goward	DOW 048:028
	Goward	DOW 048:031
	Greenan	DOW 020:063
	Legananny	DOW 033:018
	Raholp	DOW 031:004
	Saval More	DOW 047:006

Ballyreagh Dual Court Tomb, County Fermanagh

County Fermanagh		
Tomb type	Townland	SMR number
Court tombs	Aghakillymaud	FER 245:033
	Aghanaglack	FER 210:034
	Ballyreagh	FER 193:019
	Beihy	FER 243:029
	Carrickmacflaherty	FER 228:009
	Carrickmacsparrow	FER 228:013
	Cavantillycormick	FER 193:024
	Clyhannagh	FER 228:072
	Coolbuck	FER 212:060
	Cornacully	FER 209:005
	Corratrasna	FER 245:023
	Dog Big	FER 190:012
	Dog Little	FER 190:009
	Doohatty Glebe	FER 244:011
	Dromore Big	FER 135:002
	Kilnameel	FER 243:001
	Knockennis	FER 194:010
	Knockninny	FER 245:037
	Lissan	FER 212:001
	Longfield	FER 214:002
	Moylehid	FER 210:051
	Rossinure Beg	FER 190:018
	Rossinure Beg	FER 191:038
	Tawnydorragh	FER 135:001
	Tireeghan	FER 214:001
	Tully	FER 172:023
Passage tombs	Kiltierney	FER 154:002
	Moylehid	FER 210:050
Portal tombs	Glengesh	FER 194:012
	Kilrooskagh	FER 227:009
Wedge tombs	Cloghtogle	FER 212:077
	Coolbuck	FER 212:051
	Greenan	FER 244:018
	Keeran	FER 154:064
	Killy Beg	FER 190:001
	Killy Beg	FER 190:003
	Killy Beg	FER 190:006
	Meenagleragh	FER 190:017
	Mountdrum	FER 212:054
	Mountdrum	FER 212:115
	Sheemuldoon	FER 155:001

County Fermanagh		
Tomb type	Townland	SMR number
Unclassified megalithic tomb	Breagho	FER 193:021
	Brougher	FER 193:014
	Brougher	FER 193:034
	Carn	FER 193:077
	Cloghtogle	FER 212:101
	Coolbuck	FER 212:048
	Coolbuck	FER 212:052
	Coolgarran	FER 192:007
	Crocknagrally	FER 214:007
	Drummackan	FER 194:003
	Drumsloe	FER 193:081
	Garrison	FER 189:007
	Glen	FER 193:012
	Glen	FER 193:033
	Glengesh	FER 194:011
	Glengesh	FER 194:025
	Keenaghan	FER 170:009
	Killee	FER 193:009
	Killy Beg	FER 190:002
	Killy Beg	FER 190:015
	Killycreen East	FER 228:007
	Knock More	FER 191:090
	Knock More	FER 191:091
	Knock More	FER 191:092
	Knock More	FER 191:093
	Knock More	FER 191:094
	Legnavea	FER 244:031
	Legnavea	FER 244:032
	Legnavea	FER 244:033
	Lusty More Island	FER 153:018
	Meenagleragh	FER 190:020
	Mountdrum	FER 212:089
	Mountdrum	FER 212:103
	Old Barr	FER 191:086
	Ratoran	Not in SMR
	Rossinure Beg	FER 190:026
	Sheemuldoon	FER 155:003
	Slisgarrow	FER 190:019
	Tattenabuddagh	FER 214:005
	Toppan	FER 227:002

County Londonderry		
Tomb type	Townland	SMR number
Court tombs	Carrick East	LDY 017:010
	Carnanbane	LDY 030:028
	Ballygroll	LDY 023:006
	Ervey	LDY 023:007
	Clonmakane	LDY 015:034
	Knockoneill	LDY 026:052
	Tamnyrankin	LDY 026:013
	Ballybriest	LDY 045:003
	Mobuy	LDY 045:001
	Lisdillon	LDY 022:036
	Magheramore	LDY 030:064
	Mullagh	LDY 009:038
	Teeavan	LDY 031:029
Passage tomb	Moneydig	LDY 019:008
Portal tombs	Tamlaght (Coagh)	LDY 048:005
	Crevolea	LDY 011:013
	Tirnony	LDY 036:010
	Drumderg	LDY 035:002
	Clagan	LDY 029:018
	Magheramore	LDY 030:079
Wedge tombs	Ballymully	LDY 046:008
	Ballygroll	LDY 023:017
	Ballygroll	LDY 023:037
	Largantea	LDY 010:016
	Tireighter	LDY 029:001
	Carn	LDY 031:021
	Kilhoyle	LDY 017:018
	Glasakeeran	LDY 015:001
	Ballybriest	LDY 045:002
	Ballybriest	LDY 045:004
	Boviel	LDY 031:003
	Slaghtneill	LDY 032:024
	Tullybrick	LDY 040:009
Unclassified megalithic tombs	Carranroe	LDY 019:005
	Garborgle	LDY 003:058
	Carrick	LDY 016:023
	Carrick	LDY 016:024
	Crossreagh East	LDY 003:002
	Elagh More	LDY 14A:019
	Glenderowen	LDY 022:005
	Ballymully	LDY 046:042

County Londonderry		
Tomb type	Townland	SMR number
Unclassified megalithic tombs	Ballyeglish	LDY 047:041
	Cloghan	LDY 017:057
	Drumconready	LDY 036:012
	Edenreagh Beg	LDY 015:028
	Lettershendony	LDY 015:044
	Carmoney	LDY 015:025
	Gortica	LDY 014:007
	Strawmore	LDY 040:005
	Strawmore	LDY 040:008
	Tamnyreagh	LDY 015:018
	Ballynure	LDY 035:015
	Tamnyreagh	LDY 015:019
	Liscall	LDY 018:009
	Ballymoney	LDY 024:021
	Ballymoney	LDY 024:022
	Barr Cregg	LDY 023:005
	Cashel	LDY 011:005
	Clagan	LDY 029:022
	Gortfad	LDY 018:052
	Mullaboy	LDY 023:050
	Slaghtmanus	LDY 023:044
	Slaghtmanus	LDY 023:045
	Slaghtmanus	LDY 023:046
	Slaghtmanus	LDY 023:066
	Slaghtmanus	LDY 023:067
	Ballymoney	LDY 024:023
	Brockagh	LDY 015:035
	Gortmore	LDY 006:063
	Killylane	LDY 015:006
	Freugh	LDY 017:061
	Gortcorbies	LDY 010:018
	Gortgranagh	LDY 022:006
	Gortnamoyagh	LDY 018:023
	Templemoyle	LDY 030:036
	Ballymoney	LDY 024:027
	Ballymoney	LDY 024:028
	Ballymoney	LDY 024:029
	Corlacky	LDY 032:065
	Glenviggan	LDY 044:002
	Glenviggan	LDY 044:003
	Tamnyrankin	LDY 026:072
	Tullybrick	LDY 045:018

County Londonderry		
Tomb type	Townland	SMR number
Unclassified megalithic tombs	Ballybriest	LDY 045:015
	Coolnasillagh	LDY 035:009
	Dunlade Glebe	LDY 015:036
	Fallylea	LDY 032:027
	Coolnasillagh	LDY 035:011
	Mobuy	LDY 045:016
	Eden	LDY 031:026
	Cloane	LDY 035:021
	Ballydonegan	LDY 030:068
	Ballymulderg	LDY 047:045
	Ballymulligan	LDY 047:036
	Ballywoolen	LDY 003:071
	Boviel	LDY 031:038
	Carnamoney	LDY 035:014
	Carnanbane	LDY 030:077
	Carnanbane	LDY 029:043
	Carnanbane	LDY 030:076
	Carraloan	LDY 047:032
	Cluntygeeragh	LDY 031:037
	Drum	LDY 024:032
	Eden	LDY 033:030
	Fallagloon	LDY 036:045
	Feeny	LDY 030:059
	Glenshane	LDY 031:039
	Kilhoyle	LDY 017:053
	Ling	LDY 029:041
	Lisnamuck	LDY 036:022
	Loughinsholin	LDY 033:016
	Loughtilube	LDY 029:033
	Loughtilube	LDY 029:034
	Loughtilube	LDY 029:035
	Magheramore	LDY 016:030
	Mullagh	LDY 036:056
	Tamniarin	LDY 031:033
	Teeavan	LDY 031:027
	Teeavan	LDY 031:028
	Timaconway	LDY 032:052
	Tirgan	LDY 046:040

County Tyrone		
Tomb type	Townland	SMR number
Court tombs	Aghalane	TYR 027:006
	Aghnagreggan	TYR 036:020
	Ally	TYR 033:001
	Altanagh	TYR 044:045
	Altdrumman	TYR 036:032
	Altmore, alias Barracktown	TYR 045:008
	Balix Lower	TYR 006:006
	Ballywholan	TYR 065:002
	Barnes Lower	TYR 012:019
	Beltany	TYR 025:008
	Broughderg	TYR 020:006
	Carnanransky	TYR 019:005
	Carrigans	TYR 025:007
	Clady Halliday	TYR 017:023
	Clare	TYR 036:009
	Cornabracken	TYR 034:009
	Cregganconroe	TYR 037:01
	Creggandevesky	TYR 037:014
	Cullamore	TYR 065:005
	Derrydrummond	TYR 065:004
	Doocrock	TYR 049:016
	Garvagh	TYR 015:005
	Glasdrummond	TYR 060:006
	Gortnagarn	TYR 037:022
	Granagh	TYR 036:028
	Keerin	TYR 020:008
	Killeter	TYR 023:017
	Killucan	TYR 028:006
	Killymoon Demesne	TYR 038:031
	Legland	TYR 025:016
	Lisky	TYR 010:006
	Loughmacrory	TYR 027:014
	Loughmacrory	TYR 027:022
	Meenagorp	TYR 011:012
	Streefe Glebe	TYR 036:011
Passage tombs	Donaghanie	TYR 043:058
	Glenchuil	TYR 052:014
	Knockmany	TYR 059:001
	Sess Kilgreen	TYR 052:008
	Sess Kilgreen	TYR 052:012
	Sess Kilgreen	TYR 052:013

Top right: Ballyrennan Portal Tomb, County Tyrone

Right: Leitrim Portal Tomb, County Tyrone

County Tyrone		
Tomb type	**Townland**	**SMR number**
Passage tombs	Sess Kilgreen	TYR 052:040
	Shantavny Irish	TYR 052:032
Portal tombs	Altcloghfin	TYR 052:023
	Altdrumman	TYR 027:012
	Athenree	TYR 036:002
	Ballyrenan	TYR 017:035
	Ballywholan	TYR 065:003
	Bullock Park	TYR 024:029
	Carncorran Glebe	TYR 024:008
	Cashel	TYR 027:063
	Churchtown	TYR 016:018
	Cloghfin	TYR 035:007
	Creggandevesky	TYR 037:016
	Crosh	TYR 017:008
	Dullaghan	TYR 041:003
	Glenknock	TYR 017:009
	Glenroan	TYR 012:005
	Keerin	TYR 020:007
	Killynaght	TYR 005:002
	Leitrim	TYR 023:007
	Letterbratt	TYR 011:013
	Murnells	TYR 037:010
	Radergan	TYR 044:008
	Scraghy	TYR 032:004
Wedge tombs	Aghagogan	TYR 037:018
	Altdrumman	TYR 036:026
	Altmore Alias Barracktown	TYR 045:007
	Carryglass	TYR 057:010
	Churchtown	TYR 016:017
	Clogherny	TYR 011:018
	Davagh Lower	TYR 020:001
	Dunnamore, Dunamore	TYR 028:009
	Evish	TYR 005:010
	Feegarran	TYR 029:014
	Glasmullagh	TYR 025:012
	Kilknock	TYR 057:002
	Lisconrea	TYR 057:013
	Lislane	TYR 058:037
	Lislane	TYR 058:039
	Loughash	TYR 006:002

County Tyrone		
Tomb type	**Townland**	**SMR number**
	Loughash	TYR 006:024
	Loughmacrory	TYR 027:016
	Loughry	TYR 038:020
	Lurganboy	TYR 025:037
	Mullan More	TYR 036:008
	Shanmaghery	TYR 045:002
	Shantavny Scotch	TYR 052:022
	Windy Hill	TYR 002:007
Unclassified megalithic tombs	Aghafad	TYR 006:018
	Alderwood	TYR 064:037
	Ardpatrick	TYR 039:058
	Ballaghalare	TYR 005:001
	Ballynamallaght	TYR 006:034
	Ballynatubbrit	TYR 018:033
	Broughderg	TYR 020:049
	Broughderg	TYR 020:061
	Broughderg	TYR 020:055
	Broughderg	TYR 020:052
	Broughderg	TYR 020:037
	Carrickayne	TYR 006:043
	Carricklee	TYR 004:002
	Cashty	TYR 025:025
	Churchtown	TYR 017:023
	Clare Upper	TYR 024:021
	Clogherny	TYR 011:014
	Creggan	TYR 027:059
	Creggandevesky	TYR 036:037
	Creggandevesky	TYR 036:044
	Creggandevesky	TYR 037:043
	Crew	TYR 059:081
	Crouck	TYR 019:012
	Culvacullion	TYR 018:050
	Derrygoon	TYR 024:011
	Eskeradooey	TYR 018:024
	Glenroan	TYR 012:024
	Gortagammon	TYR 038:011
	Gortin	TYR 018:036
	Gortnagarn	TYR 037:047
	Keenaghan	TYR 037:006
	Killeter	TYR 023:046
	Killucan	TYR 028:005
	Knocknahorna	TYR 005:011

County Tyrone		
Tomb type	**Townland**	**SMR number**
Unclassified megalithic tombs	Leaghan	TYR 027:054
	Lettery	TYR 041:007
	Loughmacrory	TYR 027:013
	Loughmuck Alcorn	TYR 042:028
	Meaghy	TYR 016:027
	Meenacloy	TYR 032:005
	Milltown	TYR 005:004
	Moymore	TYR 037:029
	Scraghy	TYR 032:002
	Seegronan	TYR 023:001
	Seegronan	TYR 023:037
	Shanliss Lower	TYR 047:025
	Slaghtfreeden	TYR 021:002
	Sultan	TYR 037:051
	Tattykeel	TYR 029:023
	Tirconnelly	TYR 003:018
	Tirnaskea	TYR 052:035
	Turnabarson	TYR 045:016
	Urbalreagh	TYR 017:070

Photographic Credits

Photographs within this publication have been supplied by:

Chris Hill Photographic
viii-ix, 5, 11, 16, 26-27, 28, 32, 35, 36, 39, 40-41, 72, 83, 86, 107 (top)

Ken Williams
Pages iv, vi, x, 3, 7, 9, 10, 18, 21, 24, 30, 37, 38, 80, 99, 107 (bottom), 109, 115

Sam Moore
52, 81

All other photographs supplied by Gail Pollock, NIEA